THE A-Z OF CURIOUS

DERBYSHIRE

STRANGE STORIES OF MYSTERIES, CRIMES AND ECCENTRICS

RICHARD BRADLEY

The History Press

First published 2023

The History Press
97 St George's Place, Cheltenham,
Gloucestershire, GL50 3QB
www.thehistorypress.co.uk
© Richard Bradley, 2023

The right of Richard Bradley to be identified as the Author
of this work has been asserted in accordance with the
Copyright, Designs and Patents Act 1988.

All rights reserved. No part of this book may be reprinted
or reproduced or utilised in any form or by any electronic,
mechanical or other means, now known or hereafter invented,
including photocopying and recording, or in any information
storage or retrieval system, without the permission in writing
from the Publishers.

British Library Cataloguing in Publication Data.
A catalogue record for this book is available from the British Library.

978 1 8039 9040 8

Typesetting and origination by The History Press
Printed and bound in Great Britain by TJ Books Limited, Padstow, Cornwall

Contents

Acknowledgements

Thanks to Nicola Guy and Ele Craker at The History Press.

Mum, Dad, Kate, Oscar and Leo.

Lynn Burnet, David Clarke, Graham Leaver (Chesterfield Astronomical Society), Nathan Fearn, Bret Gaunt (Buxton Museum and Art Gallery), the late Michael Greatorex, Ruairidh Greig, Rod Jewell, Jean Kendall, Geoff Lester, Helen Moat, Ross Parish, Benjamin Reynolds (Media Archive for Central England), John Roper, Judy Skelton, Sam Reavey (Dronfield Heritage Trust), Matthew Hedley Stoppard and family and friends, John Widdowson.

The staff of Derbyshire Libraries, Derbyshire Record Office, University of Sheffield Special Collections.

All photographs either taken by the author or from author's collection unless otherwise indicated.

Introduction

With its stunning scenery, Derbyshire has long proved a draw for tourists and day trippers. The Peak District (often thought of as synonymous with Derbyshire in the popular consciousness, although the area it encompasses in practice also spills over into the neighbouring counties of Staffordshire, Greater Manchester, Cheshire, and South and West Yorkshire as well) was designated the UK's first National Park in 1951.

I spent the first nineteen years of my life growing up in Derbyshire (since the year 2000 I have lived just over the border in Sheffield, but pay frequent return visits), and a particular interest of mine is in the county's folklore and customs. I have previously put forward the theory – and no one has so far presented a successful counter-argument – that of all the counties in the UK, Derbyshire has the greatest density of calendar customs – ritual events that take place on a certain day each year to mark the turning of the seasons.

Some of these customs, like well dressings and the Castleton Garland ceremony, are clearly of very ancient origin. It has been speculated that these kinds of folk traditions may have survived for longer because until the railways started to penetrate Derbyshire from the mid nineteenth century onwards, the state of the roads was so infamously poor that there was a relatively low degree of population flux as people found it so difficult to get in and out of the area – hence old traditions had a greater chance to be passed down through families in a relatively 'undiluted' stock of residents.

Despite the influx of tourists into the area over the centuries, there can still be a lingering sense of insularity to some Derbyshire towns and villages to this day, making them a potent breeding ground for eccentrics – it's no coincidence that dark BBC comedy *The League of Gentlemen* decamped to the county to film the majority of their exposé of smalltown life (see Location, Location, Location).

Within the pages of *The A–Z of Curious Derbyshire* you will encounter a selection of Derbyshire's many strange 'characters' over the years, and the myriad bizarre things they have managed to get up to during their time on earth, as well as strange quirks of the landscape and local legends.

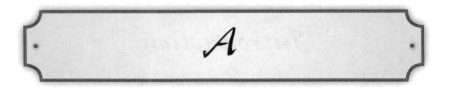

A625 ROAD

The story of the doomed A625 road begins in 1819, when the Sheffield & Chapel-en-le-Frith Turnpike Company constructed a new thoroughfare skirting the base of Mam Tor as an alternative to the nearby route through the steep-sided Winnats Pass. The name Mam Tor means 'Mother Hill' but another local nickname for the hill (which the folks at the Turnpike Company would have been advised to have paid more heed to) is the 'shivering Mountain', on account of its propensity for landslips due to unstable lower layers of shale.

The post-apocalyptic landscape of the collapsed A625 road at Castleton.

As the number of motor vehicles using the road increased in the twentieth century, the necessary closures and repairs became a regular occurrence, with major works having to be undertaken in 1912, 1933, 1946, 1952, 1966 and 1974. All efforts to shore up the road to traffic were finally abandoned in 1979 and the road was closed to cars once and for all. The decaying route remains open to walkers and cyclists, however – an unusual landmark on the outskirts of the tourist Mecca of Castleton to complement the village's several show caverns, tea rooms and souvenir shops selling the locally mined mineral Blue John.

Walking its length while avoiding the many cracks in the tarmac and sudden drops is something of an unsettling experience: it doesn't take much stretching of the imagination to envisage that you are walking through some kind of post-apocalyptic landscape. The crumbling section of A625 that remains at the base of the Shivering Mountain is a handy reminder that for all our collective ingenuity and entrepreneurship, in a game of Top Trumps, Nature would be a higher-scoring card than Humans.

B

BLACK HARRY

Black Harry was a notorious Derbyshire highwayman of the Dick Turpin mould, active on the remote moorland roads surrounding Stoney Middleton in the eighteenth century. His 'career' finally came to an abrupt end when he was captured by local law enforcers and gibbeted at Wardlow Mires. Harry's soubriquet stems from the way he used to blacken his face in order to disguise himself.

Despite his life of violent crime, terrorising people who passed through the Peaks, Black Harry has since had a degree of posthumous respectability bestowed upon him, as one of the remote country lanes above Stoney Middleton that he formerly stalked looking for suitable passing victims has had the name 'Black Harry Lane' conferred upon it. In 2011 the Black Harry Trails, a series of ten routes suitable for horse-riding and mountain-biking that converge on Black Harry Gate, were opened, having received funding from the Derbyshire

Black Harry Lane above Stoney Middleton.

Aggregate Levy Grant Scheme and support from the Peak District National Park Authority, Derbyshire County Council, landowners, residents and local businesses. These routes can nowadays be enjoyed recreationally by anyone with the desire to get out and take in the fine surrounding countryside without the threat of being asked to 'stand and deliver'.

BOGGARTS

A boggart is a North Country name for a supernatural being. The phrase was a fairly loose and adaptable one, as a boggart could take the form of a ghost, phantom dog, troll-like figure, or even a real-life flesh and blood resident of a village who was a little 'suspect' or reclusive – children were advised that they were 'boggarts' so that they would know to keep their distance. T. Brushfield, J.P., writes in his reminiscence of growing up in Ashford-in-the-Water that every 'nook or dark corner' seemed to have its own boggart, and that the boggart was invoked as 'a sort of domestic policeman, […] used to scare obedience from children, by the agency of fear', and that as well as invented supernatural phantoms, 'some old man or old woman was used as an out-door terror'.[1] Similarly, the children's authoress Alison Uttley, who grew up at Castle Top Farm near Cromford, writes of looking out of the window of the farm and seeing 'an elderly figure we called the Boggarty Man, a poor man who set traps for rabbits in the lane'.[2]

At the White Peak village of Winster there are two resident boggarts who patrol either end of the village – the Chadwick Hill or 'Chaddock' Boggart at the Elton end, and the Gurdhall, Gurdale, or 'Gurda' Boggart at the Wensley end. According to notes that Dave Bathe took down when interviewing village native Allan Stone in 1983, the Chaddock Boggart is supposed to follow you up Chadwick Hill – 'you can hear its footsteps but if you look there's nothing there – it leaves you with a hideous laugh'. Whereas the Gurdhall Boggart was 'supposed to be the ghost of the person who used to prevent children wandering away from the village – [it] stands in front of you on the road'.[3] According to the Peakland Heritage website, 'The Gurda Boggart has a long history of scaring travellers around Gurdale Farm near Winster. A young woman named Sarah Wild was once walking back home this way. Somewhere near Gurdale Farm she was accompanied for a while by "something". She could only ever describe it as "a face".'[4]

There might be a more prosaic reason for how these local legends first came into being, as Bathe's notebook records: 'Winster ghost stories – George Stone reckons that they were put around by poachers to keep people from poaching grounds at night.' (In much the same manner, many of the UK's phantom myths and legends relating to coastal areas originate from smugglers concocting and spreading stories to ensure people didn't go nosing into their hiding spots.)

After giving a talk about local folklore and customs to the Winster Local History Group in 2018 that mentioned these local boggarts, I was sent an amusing anecdote concerning the Chaddock Boggart by Lynn Burnet of the Elton Local History Group, who was present on the night: '[The Chaddock Boggart] frightened an Elton girl out of her wits in the 1950s when she was walking up the hill at night. It followed her on the other side of the wall, breathing heavily, and she could just make out an undefined ghostly white shape. It turned out to be a Friesian cow and in the dim moonlight it was only the white bits that were just visible!'[5]

At nearby Birchover, the resident boggart was called the Shale Hillock Boggart, and he lived in the Boggart Hole that was located on the New Road (B5056) between Eagle Tor and Stoney Ley Lodge. In actual fact, his 'lair' was a ventilation shaft for the Hill Carr Sough that de-watered the lead mines of Youlgrave, discharging into the River Derwent at Darley Dale. The late Birchover resident Jim Drury speculated in his memoir of village life '*Fetch the Juicy Jam!' and other Memories of Birchover*, that the Shale Hill Boggart may have been devised for practical reasons, too. Even in the 1930s, the road, with its windy bends and lack of pavement, could prove hazardous, with veteran cars, steam lorries servicing the local quarries and horses and carts all proving a potential danger to dallying pedestrians. Drury surmises that the Boggart could have been fabricated by village parents to scare their children away from playing in this dicey stretch of road.

At Brassington the local boggart conjured up to scare children into compliance was called the Sand Pit Boggart. The Kinder Boggart was one of many spirits reputed to haunt the wild moorland country around Kinder Scout in olden times.

The *Glossop Record* of 4 February 1860 reported that 'the susceptible people of Whaley [Bridge]' had been 'put into a great fear' by reports of a boggart basing itself at Shallcross Mill. The paper reported the opinions of some of the more rationally minded members of the townsfolk, who speculated that the presence may have been an otter, although the paper quashed that suggestion on the grounds of there being no fish for the hypothetical otter to eat at the mill, and concluded that 'it is the intention of the rifle corps to assemble on Saturday night about the time of its appearance, and have a shot at it'.[6] In the same paper's 15 December edition of 1866, a correspondent going by the splendidly Dickensian-sounding name of Oliver Fizzwig sketched a journey 'From Glossop To Disley and Thereabout' in which he recorded the antics of the area's notorious 'Hagg Bank Boggart', who terrorised the neighbourhood with repeated knocking. A clairvoyant was consulted, who diagnosed that the bad juju was emanating from a local resident who was radiating negative feelings towards his neighbours – but that this man would die in the early hours of the following morning. Sure enough, the clairvoyant's prediction came to pass, and the boggart activity subsequently ceased.

'Thart as fow and farse as a boggart' was given as an example of 'Popular Current Sayings of Everyday Life in Derbyshire' by the *Derbyshire Advertiser and Journal* in 1878, meaning 'You are as ugly and sly as a ghost'.[7] Boggarts were such well-known phenomena in Derbyshire in days of yore that the terminology also found its way into local place names. Gorsey Bank near Wirksworth was the location of 'Boggart's Inn' – no longer operational, although Boggart's Inn Cottage and Boggart's Inn Farm remain to the present day. A farm at Snelston was offered for sale in 1826 with various named fields, including one called 'Boggart Close', to the size of 4 acres, 2 roods and 26 perches.

Despite the fact that we now live in a more literate, scientifically minded and technologically advanced age, the influence of local boggarts has persisted in the folk memory of the area until recent times. David Clarke (2000) records that when the Planning Department of Derbyshire Dales District Council consulted local residents on a mixed use development scheme comprising shops and housing on the site of the former Cawdor Quarry on the edge of the town of Matlock in the 1990s, they received fifty replies, one of which questioned what effect the building activity would have on the site's resident Standbark Boggart. The development did subsequently suffer misfortunes, with the work dragging on interminably following the economic crash of 2008, although this can probably be laid at the door of bankers rather than boggarts.

BOWN, PHOEBE, THE 'MATLOCK AMAZON'

By the eighteenth century Matlock and Matlock Bath were both well on the way to becoming the inland tourist resorts they remain to this day, and it was in 1771 in the former town that one of Derbyshire's most remarkable characters was born. Over the course of her long lifetime (she died aged 82 in 1854), Phoebe Bown amazed both locals and tourists alike with her eccentric behaviour, but in spite of her repeated breaking of society's codes and conventions she seems to have been universally accepted by all as a local 'character'. Indeed, in her old age she even earnt the patronage of local aristocrat the Duke of Devonshire, who supplied her with an old-age pension in an era long before the welfare state introduced this same benevolent function for all and sundry (Bown's cousin's daughter had married the Duke's chief garden designer Sir Joseph Paxton, which is how she came into his orbit).

Phoebe Bown was the daughter of a local carpenter named Samuel. She seems to have inherited many of her father's practical skills, as it is said she single-handedly built an extension to her cottage to house a harpsichord she had been bequeathed. Music was another of her skills, and in addition to the harpsichord she could turn her hand to the flute, violin and cello, and played the bass-viol at Matlock's St Giles church. She was also said to have enjoyed the works of Milton, Pope and Shakespeare.

An encounter between Phoebe Bown and the Birmingham manufacturer William Hutton, when the latter was travelling through Matlock in 1801, repeatedly emphasised Bown's mannish qualities when Hutton came to write up his journey for publication in the *Gentleman's Magazine*. Her stamina for walking large distances was said to be 'more manly than a man's, and [she] can easily cover forty miles a day'. Hutton continued, 'Her common dress is a man's hat, coat, with a spencer above it, and men's shoes; I believe she is a stranger to breeches. She can lift one hundred-weight with each hand, and carry fourteen score. Can sew, knit, cook, and spin, but hates them all, and every accompaniment to the female character, except that of modesty. [...] Her voice is more than masculine, it is deep toned.' Despite laying on with a trowel how masculine Bown was in appearance and manner, Hutton goes on to reassure us that she 'has no beard'.

BRITTLEBANK VS CUDDY

The Brittlebanks were a wealthy family who, for a 200-year period from around 1700, resided at Oddo House on the outskirts of Winster, in addition to owning a large amount of land and property in the village.

In 1821 the popular local doctor William Cuddie was courting Mary Brittlebank. Mary's hot-headed brother, 27-year-old William, thought the match beneath her social standing, and after a confrontation at the doctor's house accompanied by his brothers Andrew and Francis and friend John Spencer of Bakewell (described by one newspaper report as 'another less successful admirer, it is said, of Miss Brittlebank'[8]), he engineered a duel between himself and Cuddie, which took place on the lawn of his home, Bank House, on 22 May. The outcome was that Cuddie (who appears to have been a very reluctant participant) was fatally injured.

Re-enactment of the fatal duel between William Brittlebank and William Cuddie on the lawn of Bank House, Winster, 22 May 2021.

By 1821 any romantic and heroic notions attached to duelling were fast vanishing with the changing mores of the time (the final fatal duel taking place on English soil in 1852), and the incident was viewed as cold-blooded murder. With access to so much family wealth, William Brittlebank escaped trial and the country, seemingly vanishing into thin air in a similar fashion to Lord Lucan (it is said he went to Australia). His brothers and Spencer faced trial at Derby Assizes in August 1821 for 'aiding, abetting, and assisting' in the proceedings. Such was the level of scandal caused by the events that the case was very keenly followed locally; the *Morning Post* reported that the court case 'excited an immense interest in the County. At an early hour an immense crowd surrounded the County Hall, and the rush, when the doors were opened, was tremendous.'[9] The defendants, described by the *Post* as being 'genteel and interesting young men',[10] were all found not guilty, prompting much ill feeling back in the village.

On 22 May 2021, 200 years to the day after the fatal occurrence, a troupe of Winster villagers performed a humorous re-enactment of the events leading up to the fatal duel, which was penned by local resident, retired academic and Secretary of the Winster Local History Group Geoff Lester. The play was performed in several locations around the village, culminating in a performance on the lawn of Bank House where the duel took place, with collections on the street raising £520 for the local Jigsaw foodbank charity.

BUXTON SHOE TREE

The traveller on the A515 Ashbourne Road heading out of Buxton meets a curious sight on the left-hand side of the road shortly before reaching Buxton Cemetery (perhaps you may be travelling out that way to visit the unusual grave of local antiquary Micah Salt (QV) contained within). A tree at the kerbside can be found sporting rather unusual growths – anything up to a hundred pairs of shoes dangle from its branches, twirling silently in the breeze. Some of this footwear has clearly been hanging from the tree for some time, as several have become enveloped by a mossy growth.

The photographer Sara Hannant includes a shot of the tree in her 2011 photographic survey of English rituals *Mummers, Maypoles and Milkmaids*, explaining in the accompanying text: 'Buxton teenagers created the Shoe Tree in the summer of 2006 by throwing pairs of shoes, tied together by their laces, into the highest branches of the tree. Local explanations of the shoe tree include a communal ritual, rebellion, a practical joke or to signal a drug dealer's territory.'[11]

A common phenomenon embedded within much folklore is to have a variety of competing theories spring up as to how a particular tradition came into being, but the differing explanations Hannant has collected as to the origins of the shoe tree demonstrate that this is not a trend that is solely confined to ancient customs originating hundreds of years ago in an age before mass literacy, and that despite all the advances and innovations we have seen in communications in recent years, folklore retains its power to generate a sense of mystery and legend into the twenty-first century.

A post about the tree on the local interest Facebook page 'Buxton "spatown" & District Photographs'[12] prompted a similar degree of speculation as to how and why the tree came into existence. Claims offered by way of response here ranged from it being a memorial to a young girl killed in a car crash; 'It's a form of urban graffiti, like love locks on bridges or coins in a tree stump'; 'I thought it was all the shoes that got left behind when people have stayed at Duke's Drive camp site'; and 'I thought it was an old wives tale that hanging shoes in a certain tree would help with fertility'.

One local commented, 'It was started by a gentleman who had lived in Tasmania and came to live close by … [who] passed away recently' – a theory that appears to be corroborated with a degree of authority (although a variance as to the place of inspiration) by a subsequent comment: 'My late father-in-law, Peter Wren, started that shoe tree. When he was visiting New Zealand he saw one there and basically he thought it will be a good idea to start [the] tradition

Strange fruit: Buxton Shoe Tree.

here.' If this is indeed the true story as to how the Buxton tree came to sprout so many pairs of shoes, then it turns out to be a custom that has been imported to Derbyshire soil from the opposite side of the globe.

In addition to the wide variety of theories as to why it is there, this strange landmark is by no means universally popular among Buxtonians, the same Facebook post drawing comments from townsfolk along the lines of, 'A DAMN Eyesore. Cut it down' (which to me seems a little unfair on the tree, which didn't really have a great degree of choice in the matter), 'I think it's an eyesore & cruel to the tree. I'd like to take them all down', and, 'It's littering of course'.

CRANTSES, OR MAIDEN'S GARLANDS

A 'crants', also known as a 'maiden's garland', is a relic from a bygone age, formerly produced whenever a young unmarried (and therefore, in theory – if the societal conventions of the time had been adhered to – virginal) girl of the community passed away. They consist of delicate paper-hooped garlands that were carried ahead of the coffin at the funeral and subsequently suspended from the roof of the church. The word 'crants' is believed to be of Scandinavian origin and the practice is referenced in Shakespeare's *Hamlet*, when it is said of Ophelia, 'Yet here she is allow'd her virgin crants, Her maiden strewments and the bringing home Of bell and burial', suggesting that the custom was known of in England since at least Tudor times.

These garlands were formerly a widespread sight across Derbyshire, with records of them once having hung at the churches of Eyam, Glossop, Hathersage, Heanor, Hope, Fairfield, Tissington, Ashover, Bolsover, West Hallam, Darley Dale, Ilkeston (where 'fifty or more' were said to have hung in the mid-1800s), Crich and South Wingfield (the latter survived into the twentieth century, but was destroyed under the instruction of a churchwarden named William Brighouse on the grounds that it was 'nothing but a dust harbourer').

It is a pity that this particular garland has not survived, as it has a story attached to it. In the eighteenth century the landlord of The Peacock Inn at Oakerthorpe was Peter Kendall, who was also a churchwarden at the parish church at South Wingfield. Kendall had a beautiful daughter named Ann who was courted by a young local farmer. Ann subsequently fell pregnant by the farmer but upon discovering this news the ungallant chap swiftly ditched her. Ann gave birth to a baby daughter but in view of the mores of her era she was said to be so affected by the shame and scandal that she subsequently died of a broken heart in 1745. At her funeral a garland was dutifully produced in her memory and hung in the church, until it fell foul of Brighouse's aesthetic sensibilities. The farmer who failed to accept the consequences of his actions is said to have got his comeuppance one day while riding his horse past the

A couple of the crantses normally kept in storage at St Giles Church, Matlock.

church shortly after Ann's burial. The church bells suddenly and unexpectedly began to clang out, causing his horse to rear up in surprise, which threw him to the ground, causing death by a broken neck.

When this particular local story is retold, the farmer's name is said to be unknown – perhaps the moral being that such caddish behaviour consigns you to oblivion and you don't deserve to have your name recorded for posterity in the history books. While as a folklorist I hate to debunk a good folk tale, I did come across Anne (not Ann, as most tellings of the story have it) Kendall's entry on ancestry.com.[13] It tells us that she was born in South Wingfield on 1 November 1713, and did indeed die there in 1745 – as did her mother, Mary Kendall née Flint, thus making 1745 a doubly tragic year for Peter; did the scandal also finish off Mary as well? The record says that Anne's daughter was named Ann Kendall (this time minus the 'e') and that she was born in 1745, with the date of her death unknown. Intriguingly, in Anne's entry we also have a spouse listed – a Thomas Dodd. Could this be our unchivalrous farmer? If so, contrary to the accepted version of events, did they marry after all? Or was Kendall married to Dodd and having an extra-marital affair with the farmer? Dodd does not have either a birth or death date recorded alongside his name, thus giving us no further clues as to his identity.

Crants on display at Holy Trinity Church, Ashford-in-the-Water.

The antiquarian magpie Thomas Bateman of Lomberdale Hall near Middleton-by-Wirksworth, an enthusiastic archaeologist frequently to be found digging into prehistoric burial sites in the surrounding Peakland countryside, acquired a pair of garlands from St Giles at Matlock and placed them in his private museum within his house for posterity. A 1911 *Folklore* article stated that some from the same church had been sold to tourists as 'curiosities'.

Happily, St Giles still has a handful of crantses in its possession – one of which has been restored thanks to funding from the Churches Council and placed on display in a glass case in the vestry, with a further five kept in archival storage boxes. On a fieldwork visit to St Giles, churchwarden Brian Legood kindly retrieved three of the examples from storage that are not normally on display for me to photograph, as can be seen in the photo reproduced on the previous page.

Nowadays, in addition to the Matlock crantses, the only surviving examples of this touching custom within Derbyshire are to be found at the churches of Ashford-in-the-Water, Trusley, and Ilam on the Derbyshire–Staffordshire border. Whilst the Derbyshire examples are particularly well documented, it was not a custom that was unique to the area, with other surviving crantses to be found elsewhere in the country at churches at Beverley, East Yorkshire; Robin Hood's Bay, North Yorkshire; Springthorpe, Lincolnshire; and Abbots Ann in Hampshire.

DERBY TUP

A large stone sculpture of a ram by Michael Pegler can be found on East Street in Derby commemorating the Derby Ram or Derby Tup, a 'tup' being an old dialect word meaning an uncastrated male ram. This fabulous beast of gigantic proportions is the subject of a supremely catchy folk song. So catchy, in fact, that it was known across the globe – a correspondent to *Notts and Derbyshire Notes and Queries* claimed that George Washington once took the twin sons of Chief Justice Ellsworth of Connecticut, placed one on each knee, and sang the song of the Derby Ram to them – I wonder if Joe Biden could reel it off?

The Derby Ram statue by Michael Pegler on East Street in Derby.

Writing in *The Ballads of Derbyshire* (published 1867), Llewellynn Jewitt noted:

> The origin of this popular old ballad has yet to be ascertained. At present it
> has puzzled more heads than one, and its elucidation must be left to future
> research. Its principal characteristic is its bold extravagance. Derby and Derby
> people have, however, I know by references to allusions to it, been fond of
> their Ram for more than a century. How much older it is than that time is
> difficult to say.[14]

It certainly dates to an era long pre-dating genetic modification in the meat
industry, but regarding that 'bold extravagance', the song is a masterpiece of
darkly comic hyperbole, featuring a surreally large sheep with eyes as big as
footballs and wool upon its back that reaches up to the sky so that eagles nest
in it. The opportunistic butcher who attempts to slaughter this giant beast gets
his comeuppance as he gets washed away by a flood of its blood.

Up until the 1980s, during the Christmas and New Year period it was
common to see small groups of teenagers (usually boys) performing a
mummers play based around the song in the pubs and miners' welfare clubs
in the area around the Derbyshire–Nottinghamshire–South Yorkshire borders.
One member of the team would act out the part of the Tup, fashioning a
sheep costume out of whatever materials were available, and being ritually
'slaughtered' by the butcher character.

Soon after the publication of Jewitt's ballads book, the *Derbyshire Times* of
2 January 1869 reported on the festivities in the streets of Chesterfield on
Christmas Eve 1868, where various carol singing and mumming groups were
seen performing as well as 'a lot of youngsters who glory in the traditional
"Oud Tup O' Darby" [sic]'.[15]

The play features recurring characters: the Man, Our Owd Lass (the
Man's wife), the Butcher and the Tup itself, sometimes accommodating extra
characters depending on the size of the team. This would be performed around
Christmas and New Year's Eve, usually by adolescent boys, in local pubs and
clubs, in the streets and house-visiting door to door, and a collection taken
after the performance. As the performers got older, the song and play would
be passed down to younger generations of local lads – sometimes younger
brothers of previous performers – and would almost always be learnt orally,
with no written scripts existing.

A wonderful record of the Tup in its heyday survives in the form of the
1974 film *The Derby Tup*, produced for Garland Films by folk music and dance

scholar Ian Russell and the late Barry Callaghan, filmmaking tutor at Sheffield Polytechnic, who was also heavily involved in folk music. The film is included on the BFI's DVD release *Here's a Health to the Barley Mow*, a compendium of archive footage of folklore events from around the UK.

The film documents the 1971 team at Ridgeway on the Derbyshire– South Yorkshire border preparing for and giving a performance, followed by a completely new team taking over and performing the custom in 1972. The ways in which the sheep costume is improvised are discussed – it could comprise a turnip on a stick and an old coat, incorporate a genuine sheep's skull, or simply be a performer crouched under an old blanket. The prop Tup used at Ridgeway is described in the commentary as a 'more splendid and permanent creation' carved from oak and with flashing eyes supplied by torches, which at the time of filming was around twenty years old, having been passed down through various teams who inherited custodianship of the custom. The same Tup can be seen being used twenty years down the line in a video shot by folklorist Peter Bearon of the Ridgeway team performing on New Year's Eve 1995 at Marsh Lane and Ford, near Eckington (but where is it now? Lurking in someone's attic?).

At the end of Russell and Callaghan's film the 1972 team are shown dividing up their considerable collection money gained from performing the Tup in the local pubs and clubs.

In addition to the film, Russell, who at the time was living at Unstone near Dronfield, conducted extensive fieldwork research into the custom throughout the 1970s, when it was flourishing in surrounding communities in north-east Derbyshire. The results were published in the 1979 volume of *Folk Music Journal*, where detailed studies were made of performances by groups from Barrow Hill, Birdholme, Bolsover, Brimington, Creswell, Eckington, Harthill, Killamarsh, Middle Handley, Poolsbrook, Renishaw, Ridgeway, Stanfree and Unstone.

In Barrow Hill, to witness the Tup in action was viewed as bringing good luck to the spectator. Russell records women touching the Tup costume for luck, and one woman who arrived at a venue just after a performance had concluded being so distraught at having missed the Tup that she insisted on accompanying them to their next venue to witness it to ensure luck for the forthcoming new year. The same Barrow Hill Tup team performed in 1975 to a large audience at the Aquarius, Chesterfield's former incongruously glitzy nightclub on Whittington Moor.

It is clear from Russell's article that the performance of the Derby Tup at Christmas and New Year was a huge part of the cultural fabric of midwinter festivities in north-east Derbyshire, and an important rite of passage for its young performers. And yet, within the space of a generation, this custom has all but died out. Why? Folklorist Ross Parish, author of the 'In Search of Traditional Customs and Ceremonies' blog, sees an overlapping multitude of reasons. Firstly, an increased cultural sensitivity to the mistreatment of animals, as manifested in the rise of vegetarianism, veganism and environmentalism. Another factor being the much greater range of entertainment teenagers can access by comparison to the 1970s, combined with increased affluence – 'children are less likely to find ways to raise their own money if they don't need to', Parish observes – and what in the 1970s may have been viewed as youthful entrepreneurship in collecting money after a performance that the participants kept for themselves may now be looked down on as 'begging' because of cultural shifts. 'This combined with "stranger danger" probably sealed the fate of the original run of the custom – many people could not imagine their young children travelling around pubs to collect money and be concerned, rightly so, for their safety.'[16]

The geographical reach of the Derby Tup in its heyday spread beyond the county border into neighbouring South Yorkshire and north Nottinghamshire. You can still see the Tup being performed to this day but are much more likely to witness it in South Yorkshire, where three known groups keep the tradition alive: the Handsworth Sword Dancers, Harthill Morris and Lord Conyers Morris Men. The majority of the performers from these folk dance spin-off groups are middle-aged, and not the teenage boys who were formerly the custodians of the custom.

In 2021 I made contact with Matthew Hedley Stoppard. A native of Clay Cross, Matthew is, like myself, fascinated by local customs and folklore, and in 2020 published through Valley Press *The Garland King*, his collection of poetry inspired by strange Derbyshire and other UK traditions. I had seen on Matthew's Instagram page (@mhstoppard) that he had exported a Derbyshire custom to the West Yorkshire town of Otley where he now lives, performing the Derby Tup with members of his family at Christmas 2020. Matthew describes himself as 'a proud Derbyshireman' and the Derby Tup is his favourite mummers' play and folk song, therefore 'performing it in deepest West Yorkshire is all part of my missionary work'.

Despite having grown up in north-east Derbyshire, Matthew had never witnessed the Tup being performed locally first-hand. He drew on Russell and Callaghan's film for inspiration for a performance involving his wife and two sons Ted and Fran, explaining:

Lord Conyers Morris Men performing the Derby Tup at the Wales Jubilee Social Club, South Yorkshire, in December 2017.

Our Tup revival followed a performance of the St George's mummers' play, which we prepared and performed in April 2020 in the middle of the street, in the middle of the first [Covid-19] lockdown, to entertain our older neighbours. Pre-pandemic we had found a sheep's skull at the side of the river and this became our Tup (after a thorough clean) when we performed it just before Christmas 2020. We performed it three times on the night and the majority of the neighbours loved it and had lots of questions about the play's origins. Some small children were a bit unsettled by the skull and the glowing eyes I had made out of a pre-coded BBC Micro:bit, borrowed from Leeds Libraries.

On 27 November 2020, Matthew gave a reading of his poems at Chesterfield Labour Club as part of the 'Independent Electric Group presents' event, along with 'an interactive version of The Derby Tup, inviting members of the audience to take part'. This performance by Matthew, his pals and audience members could well have marked the first time the Tup has been performed in Chesterfield (perhaps the whole of Derbyshire) for thirty or forty years – well done on reviving a lapsed Derbyshire tradition, Matthew!

Matthew Hedley Stoppard and friends revive the Tup at Chesterfield Labour Club, November 2021.

Despite the dearth of local performances, the Derby Tup's legacy lives on within the county: a pub at Whittington Moor popular with Chesterfield FC fans, the former Brunswick Hotel, has been renamed The Derby Tup. In addition to Pegler's statue, Derby also has Wilfred Edgar Dudeney's bronze 'Boy and Ram' sculpture on display, commissioned for an indoor shopping centre but later relocated to the city's River Gardens. And in summer 2021, a series of thirty 5ft-high Derby rams painted by different artists graced the streets of Derby, subsequently being auctioned to raise money for Derby Museums. Most pleasing of all, on a visit to Derby's St George's Day festivities in 2017, I spotted a child carrying a homemade Derby Tup effigy constructed of a broom handle, shoebox and – yes! – footballs for eyes.

THE DEVIL IN DERBYSHIRE

Derbyshire has long been a popular tourist spot within the United Kingdom, with people travelling to sites such as Buxton and Matlock Bath for recreational relaxation since at least the sixteenth century. One of the more surprising visitors to the county over the years is the dark lord Satan himself, who would appear to have a particular fondness for the area given that he keeps making return visits – in spite of the majority of his day trips to Derbyshire usually resulting in some form of humiliation.

Chesterfield's crooked-spire church – or, to give it is formal name, the Parish Church of St Mary and All Saints – has become an iconic image and thoroughly embraced as the town's logo, appearing on council street signs and produce manufactured in the town ranging from Northern Tea Merchants tea to pickled onions, as well as lending the town's football team their nickname of The Spireites. Sober-minded architectural historians will tell you that the spire acquired its kink as a result of the lead plates used on the roof being attached to unseasoned timber and warping in the sun – possibly as a result of a lack of skilled workers in the wake of the Black Death, which had been ravaging the country in the fourteenth century (the spire is believed to have been added to the existing church building sometime around the year 1362).

Folklorists, however, will spin you far more colourful yarns as to how the church roof came to be bent out of shape, several of which involve the Devil. One story runs that the Devil was having his hooves shod by a blacksmith in the town of Bolsover located 6 miles to the east of Chesterfield. The cack-handed blacksmith drove his nail too far into the Devil's hoof, causing him to fly off in pain; he clipped the spire in his haste and confusion as he was flying over Chesterfield and it has remained bent out of shape ever since.

Another story has it that the Devil was perched atop the weathervane on the spire roof when incense used in a holy rite wafted up from the church below, causing the Devil to sneeze violently, which caused the warping of the spire. Yet another Devilish take on how the spire came to be malformed sees the Devil resting on top of it while flying between Nottingham and Sheffield; the ringing of the church bells so startles him that he flies off abruptly, disfiguring the roof in the process.

Chesterfield's iconic crooked spire: is the Devil responsible for its kink?

My own personal favourite folk legend concerning how the spire developed its kink has nothing to do with the Devil, however – a rival theory runs that one day at the church a rumour went around that a Chesterfield bride who was getting married remained in a state of virginity on her wedding day – the spire itself was so surprised at this rare occurrence that it twisted itself around to have a good look at this pure lady of Chesterfield and has remained disfigured ever since …

Muggington near Ashbourne is the location of the Halter Devil Chapel, a tiny (13ft 9in × 17ft 7in) building attached to a farmhouse that can accommodate around thirty people, founded by local man Francis Brown in 1723. Brown was something of a rum 'un, being accused of misappropriating public funds and a notoriously hard drinker. One dark and stormy night while characteristically smashed out of his face, he attempted to halter his horse in order to ride to Denby to procure some coal. Brown's inebriated state combined with his horse's skittishness in response to the thunder and lightning to make this something of a fool's errand. Eventually, in frustration, Brown is said to have cried out angrily, 'If I can't halter thee, I'll halter the Devil!' At which point, an almighty flash of lightning illuminated the presence with him in the field of a large horned figure. Terrified, Brown vowed on the spot to mend his recalcitrant ways and subsequently had the chapel built, becoming a pious law abider thereafter. Of course, the horned figure he saw that drunken and dramatic night may well have been a local cow – but who are we to let these small details get in the way of a good epiphany story?

Wayne Anthony in *Haunted Derbyshire* relates an ancient legend that the siting of St Alkmund's Church at Duffield was influenced by the Devil, in a rare instance of him getting his own way. The church builders had chosen a spot close to the site of Duffield Castle, intending to reuse some of the materials from the ruined fortress formerly belonging to the de Ferrers family, who were once Earls of Derby. Upon returning to the site on the second day of work, the builders found that all their work the previous day had mysteriously been undone and the materials moved to a different site at the opposite end of the village. They transported them back to the original site, only to find the following morning that the same thing had happened. According to the superstitions of the time, it was thought the Devil was responsible for this meddling and so prayers were incanted at the building site to try to put a stop to it. However, this did not work and after a week of frustrated attempts the builders finally gave up and built the church at the site that it now occupies close to the River Derwent. According to one telling, the Devil's motivation was that he didn't want the church to occupy such a prominent position on the hilltop site as originally intended, as it might attract too many 'customers' who were in opposition to him and all he stood for …

One of Castleton's many caverns that has been open to the public for several centuries goes by the name of 'Devil's Arse'. It had been known by this name since at least 1586, when it appears in William Camden's *Britannia* as a noteworthy local feature of the district. The name was changed to the more genteel 'Peak Cavern' in 1880 as Queen Victoria was due to visit and the owners didn't want to cause offence to the monarch – although given that it has been often speculated that both that she used cocaine and marijuana and her husband is supposed to have had a genital piercing to which he lent his name, one would have thought she would have been broad-minded enough to cope with the original name. It has in recent years reverted back to its older, more attention-grabbing name; when my 10-year-old son and his classmates visited Castleton recently for a school residential trip, the class were instructed by the teachers to look the other way when walking past a large sign advertising the attraction!

In a more superstitious age, people believed that the caverns were a direct route to Hell. But where does the arse part come into it? Well, in a similar situation to that which caused the 'Mad Dog' legend at Jughole Cave (QV) to originate, at a certain point in the cave network, under the right conditions, water collects and ebbs and flows in a small cavity in the rock formation, causing slurping and sucking noises that reverberate around the cavern, and an earlier generation of cavern explorers took this to be the noise of the Devil farting, hence the name.

Near Coxbench in the vicinity of Castle Farm can be found the Devil's Shovel Full – a name popularly ascribed to a large circular earthwork mound. The story behind the name is that the Devil was travelling this way with characteristically mischievous intent – he was carrying a large shovel full of earth that he intended to tip into the River Derwent at Derby and dam it. However, en route he lost one of his shoes and was forced to dump the earthy contents of the shovel so he could fully focus on locating it, creating the tumulus that has remained to this day in the process.

A legend dating back to medieval times ventures that the Hemlock Stone, a large outcrop of New Red Sandstone at Stapleford in the neighbouring county of Nottinghamshire, was deposited there by the Devil, who threw it from atop a hill in Castleton (a distance of around 35 miles as the crow flies) in annoyance at the ringing of the church bells there.

A common Derbyshire belief cited by Armitage in *Derbyshire Fare* is that if harvesting wild blackberries, you should be sure to pick them before Michaelmas Day, 29 September, because on this day the Devil poisons the fruit by going round either spitting or urinating on them, which naturally spoils the flavour. Jim Drury of Birchover provides us with more information regarding the origin of this superstition: 'An old wife's tale says that jam made with blackberries picked after Michaelmas Day will not set. For it is the day that St Michael threw the Devil out of Heaven – he landed in a bramble patch and in his rage he p….d on the plant.' Drury goes on to provide a slightly more scientific reason for how this belief came to be: 'Actually there is often a frost in late September that destroys the pectin in the fruit.'[17]

DRAGONS

If it's not one thing, it's another: if Derbyshire's residents in days of yore weren't being menaced by the dark lord on one of his frequent day trips to the county, they were having to fend off attacks by dragons.

There are plenty of accounts of these fabulous fire-breathing beasts having visited the county over the years – and for a guaranteed dragon sighting, there are several tangible representations still to be found in the fabric of Derbyshire's churches and buildings.

Dragons on the streets of Chesterfield: one pays a visit during the town's annual Medieval Fun Day.

According to local folk tales, the Matlock area had its own local resident dragon. John Farey's *General View of the Agriculture and Minerals of Derbyshire*, published in three volumes between 1811 and 1817 and running to almost 2,000 pages, is in general as dull as its title suggests – apart from a short but fascinating section covering the 'Customs, Opinions, Amusements, &c. of the People' of Georgian-era Derbyshire. Farey was informed by Matlock citizens whom he encountered on his travels that young children of the district were made to 'stare and tremble' by warnings from older relatives concerning the town's dragon.

This is presumably the same dragon who crops up in Ruth Tongue's *Folk Tales of the English Counties*, published in 1970 and compiled from oral folktales collected by Tongue dating back as far as the 1920s – although here the dragon's realm has shifted a few miles northwards toward Chesterfield.

Tongue supplies two separate versions of the dragon legend. In the first, the dragon is defeated by a priest climbing 'Winlatter Rock' in the surrounding countryside. The priest assumes the shape of a cross as the dragon flies over, an act that takes so much willpower that his feet sink into the rock. I have not managed to locate Winlatter Rock on any maps.

In version two, the moral of the story is the value of teamwork. 'Three Valiant Lads', who are brothers, commission a blacksmith to make a huge sword, which they carry up to Winlatter Rock. Being repeatedly told of the impossibility of defeating the dragon by all they encounter, their stock response is that 'one can't but three can'. When the dragon approaches, at a given signal the church bells of Chesterfield and Grindleford are rung and the giant sword brandished. The monster is so disorientated by this sensory overload, it disappears off into a Blue John mine, never to be seen again (Visit Derbyshire & Peak District will surely be delighted at the shoehorning in of one of the county's showpiece attractions just before the conclusion of the tale).

The legend of the dragon persisted into the late twentieth century. Darley Dale schoolteacher Ernest Paulson, writing in the March 1981 issue of *Derbyshire Life*, claimed that every year when he taught in Matlock schools he was asked by his latest cohort of pupils whether there was a monster dwelling under Masson Hill. Paulson, who in addition to his day job was a keen local historian, sets down the legend of the dragon in his article, which combines the gist of both versions recorded by Tongue and is then garnished with some additional local flavour. Here in place of the priest who climbs Winlatter Rock, it is the hermit living in the cave at Cratcliffe Tor near Birchover who performs this act – on the Fabrick Rock, near Ashover. This hermit existed in real life; surviving kitchen notes from Haddon Hall record a payment in 1549 made to 'Ye Harmytt' on 23 December for supplying the kitchen with ten rabbits, as well as earning an additional fourpence for guiding people to Haddon. After the hermit's death, however, the dragon returns and resumes causing mayhem – which is where the three brothers step in with their giant sword.

In Paulson's telling, the defeated dragon subsequently goes to ground in Jughole Cave above Snitterton. From this base he makes the dragon the root cause of some of the geological phenomena of the local area, suggesting that the fiery breath it expels while exiled in the cave is responsible for heating the warm thermal springs of Matlock Bath, and flames which shoot out of the hillside at Riber, disturbing the rocks. Finally, according to Paulson, 'when he twitches his tail, as he does from time to time, people say that there is an earthquake and houses fall in Winster'. Presumably this is a reference by Paulson to the Winster Tremors, a series of earth shocks that struck the White Peak village in the twentieth century that caused pictures to fall off cottage walls, chimney stacks to topple into the street and masonry to fall off the village church, more likely caused by all the lead mining activity in the area over the years.

A common role ascribed to dragons in British folklore is as guardians of buried treasure. This appears to be the case at the parish of Drakelow in south Derbyshire. The place name, first recorded in AD 942, means 'Dragon's Mound', but just what treasure the resident dragon is supposed to be guarding within its hilly lair has been lost in the mists of time. However, when excavation work on the now-demolished Drakelow Power Station 'C' was taking place in 1962, a small carved Anglo-Saxon vessel dated to around AD 550 and now in the collections of Derby Museum was discovered, indicating the presence of a ceremonial burial mound.

The High Peak village of Wormhill suggests a similar place name origin; the English Place-Name Society, however, put their money on 'Wyrma's Hyll', 'Wyrma' being a person. However, a giant worm can be interchangeable with a dragon in British folklore (see, for example, the story of The Lambton Worm of County Durham). And dragons are never too far away in Wormhill: it's been suggested a standing stone on private land in the grounds of a farmhouse (visible from the roadside) features a now-weathered carving of a dragon's head, and in St Margaret's Church can be found a carving of the saint with a dragon. Meanwhile, the terraced banks of Knotlow Hill are said to have been formed by the dragon coiling its tail around the land.

Another hill connected with dragons can be found close to the Staffordshire border, where the ridge of Chrome Hill near Earl Sterndale is popularly known as the 'Dragon's Back' due to its resemblance to a slumbering beast.

Brassington has a road named Dragon Hill. Even genteel Baslow has a cave known as Wormstall Edge or Dragon's Hole, which travellers were advised to avoid.

Dragons show up in the lead mining industry that was formerly widespread across the White Peak area. It was the custom for the miners to stake their claim for the lead workings they had discovered by naming them, the results often having a strange poetry and fantastical imagery of their own. Near Bonsall there is a mine called Fiery Dragon and there are at least three examples of mines named Burning Drake.

Dragons also appear with surprising regularity in sculpted form in the stonework of churches – perhaps symbolising the old Pagan religions that were supplanted by Christianity. A fine example can be found at the Church of St John the Baptist at Ault Hucknall, in what appears to be a tympanum over a former, now walled-up, entrance. This scene has been interpreted as St George battling a dragon – although the church guide booklet observes that the man's armour appears of the Norman era and therefore pre-dates the adoption of St George as the patron saint of England in the fourteenth century (the church dates from the eleventh century), and suggests that the figure may in fact represent St Michael the Archangel expelling the dragon from heaven.

Dragon carving on the stonework of St John the Baptist Church, Ault Hucknall.

Dragon carved in the woodwork of St John the Baptist Church, Tideswell.

Other dragon carvings in Derbyshire churches can be found at Darley Dale, Tideswell, Swarkestone, on Parwich's tympanum and the font at Ashford-in-the-Water, on the lintel above the door at Birchover, and on a medieval cross shaft at Sandiacre Church, discovered buried under the pulpit during renovation work in 1854 and now set into the floor of the chancel. Derby Museum has on display a ninth-century Anglo-Saxon stone cross shaft that was discovered in 1844 when the original (now demolished) St Alkmund's church was being renovated. It depicts a number of fabulous birds and beasts, including a dragon.

Elsewhere at Derby, a lovely sculpted clock can be found close to the railway station ornamented with several wyverns – a close relative of the dragon that was used as the symbol of the Midland Railway company. The company chose the beast, which also adorned branded items such as cutlery and crockery and was worn as a silver badge by employees, claiming it to be symbol of the ancient kingdom of Mercia whose land their tracks criss-crossed (although their early steam trains must also have borne a passing coincidental resemblance to these fire-breathing beasts as they tore across the country belching out smoke). The clock formerly adorned the entrance to the Midland Station, but when the original frontage was demolished in 1985 it was rescued and re-sited: it now finds itself somewhat marooned in the corner of a nearby car park.

A further secular dragon carving can be found in the windowsill of an old house at Hopton, which is now quite weathered, but once again seems to show the dragon in battle with a knight. A less ancient bas-relief on the George and Dragon Inn at Ashbourne depicts St George on horseback fighting a dragon, dramatically advertising the establishment.

The church at Elton has an unusual carving on the font, showing a dragon-like beast, although it is another close cousin, a salamander – not the small amphibian to which family newts belong, but in the folklore world a more fabulous beast entirely that could also breathe fire and additionally emit poison.

In 1805 the spire of Elton church collapsed and fell in on the rest of the building, destroying it (it has been speculated the local lead miners had not respected the mining laws that forbade prospecting in churchyards, and by illicitly digging around the church had weakened its foundations). A whole new replacement church had to be built, which opened in 1812. Elton's font, which had been damaged when the spire fell in, ended up languishing outdoors in the churchyard while the rebuilding was taking place – and beyond. In 1838 it was spotted by the Reverend Pidcock, the vicar of nearby Youlgrave, who took a fancy to it and whimsically placed it in the rectory garden as an ornamental feature. His slightly more clued-up successor, the Reverend Wilmot, knew the difference between a valuable medieval font and a birdbath, and had it installed inside the church at Youlgrave in 1848. Under closer scrutiny the font turned out to be an extreme rarity, perhaps unique, being a medieval font incorporating a stoup (a spout-like protuberance that held oil at baptism ceremonies, or holy water). When the villagers of Elton realised they had carelessly lost a rare piece of their heritage they tried to reclaim the font, but the vicar of Youlgrave would not entertain the idea, having by now restored it with a new base. The lord of the manor, William Pole Thornhill of nearby Stanton Hall, tried to soften the blow by commissioning an exact replica of the original font in 1870, which is the one that now sits in Elton church.

I gave a talk on local folklore and customs to the Elton Local History Group in 2018, and during the question and answer session afterwards I had a question of my own to put to the Eltonions. I had collected various colourful references to the bitter ongoing local rivalry between the neighbouring villages of Elton and Winster (*see* Rivalries). I was keen to know, were things really as bad as people always made out?

'Yes,' thundered a voice from the back of the village hall, 'and with Youlgrave it's even worse. We still haven't forgiven them for the font!'

ELEPHANTS

In 1896, elephant bones along with those belonging to hippopotamus and rhinoceros were discovered in the gravel of the Derwent at Allenton, near Derby. You probably don't need me to point out that elephants are nowadays a non-native species to Derbyshire; however, they have sometimes paid a visit to the area over the years, in one notable case causing chaos in their wake.

The image of an elephant with the quasi-exotic name of 'Namunah' can be spotted on the mock-Tudor gable end on the rear of a building in Matlock that at the time of writing forms the premises of the Nationwide Building Society (the carving is best viewed from the town's Hall Leys Park). Its presence is a historic hangover from the building's former use as Burgon's grocery stores, the elephant being the chain's trademark. Originally this elephant took the form of a three-dimensional wooden carving; unfortunately, in the early years of the twenty-first century while repair work was being carried out on the building, Namunah, who was by now almost a hundred years old, disintegrated upon being removed from the wall. A two-dimensional silhouette version was painted on the wall in the same spot to retain the connection with the building's history.

An interesting curio from film history is preserved in the BFI national film archive and is available to watch for free on the BFI's 'Britain on Film' map, an excellent online resource that pinpoints regional archive films dating back to the earliest days of moving images to their filming location on a map. The film, which appears under the title *Evidence*, is an interesting historical record of the townscape of Chesterfield in 1935 – despite the fact that we are now well into the twentieth century by the time the footage was shot, there are still plenty of horse-drawn carts rushing by on business, and most of the men in the crowd are sporting *Peaky Blinders*-style flat caps.

This film's historic importance that has earnt it a place on the BFI film map, however, stems from the fact that this footage marks the first time that covert filming was used as evidence in a British court case. *Evidence* records the illicit gambling activities of a gang of illegal street bookmakers, and was used

Namunah's silhouette on gable end of former Burgon's grocery stores, Matlock.

successfully to bring about their conviction. The *Derbyshire Times* report[18] under the headline 'Remarkable Court Scenes – Film Shown of Betting Offences – Smart Work by Chesterfield Police' described the novelty of the situation for defendants and magistrates alike when Chesterfield Court House was 'temporarily turned into a cinema':

> Chesterfield is the first town in the country to show a cinematograph film to magistrates in a police court. This unprecedented course was taken on Wednesday by the Chesterfield Borough Police in connection with alleged street betting offences in the Market Place, Chesterfield, on April 30th and May 1st, in respect of which 39 men were charged. The court was temporarily turned into a cinema. The windows were specially darkened and the projector was erected on a table across the top of the dock, the screen being placed against the wall on the opposite side of the room. A police officer operated the apparatus, while another officer acted as commentator. [...] The film was approximately 300 feet in length and took 15 minutes to run through quickly. It was shown a second time at a slower speed and was repeatedly stopped on the call of a defendant who wished to question certain of the scenes.

Our everyday business being captured by surveillance cameras is a commonplace fact of life nowadays, and the footage that they record is routinely used in court cases – but it is Chesterfield Police who can claim to be the pioneers here. After a hearing that lasted for eight and a half hours, fourteen out of the thirty-nine accused ended up being convicted, landing fines ranging from £2 to £20. Advances in technology have meant that miniaturised bugging devices can now covertly record people's actions with ease, but back in 1935 PC Saunders of Chesterfield Borough Police had to secrete himself and a bulky movie camera in the first floor of a building overlooking the Market Place, where he spent a week unobserved capturing the activities of the bookmakers. According to the newspaper, the novelty of the situation was not lost on those present, including the accused in the dock:

> During the showing of the film, comments – humorous and otherwise – were heard from many of the defendants. One was heard to say, 'Who's going to pay the – entertainment tax? [a tax on cinemagoing introduced by the UK Government in 1916 which was abolished in 1960]' – Another was heard to ask 'Were you in the ninepenny or the fourpenny seats?'[19]

You might very well by now be wondering what all this has got to do with elephants. Well, adding a nicely surreal touch to this piece of British legal and cinematic history, at one point the footage is unexpectedly gatecrashed by a troop of elephants ambling into the frame and making their way through the Market Place – they happened to be performing in a circus that was visiting Chesterfield at the time of PC Saunders' surveillance. Their impromptu appearance in the footage was another cause of mirth in the courtroom, as the *Derbyshire Times* noted: 'There were occasions when the defendants laughed loudly at certain incidents in the film, particularly when three elephants, who were performing at a circus in the town, ambled slowly across the screen.'[20]

A less comical visit by a circus elephant to Derbyshire occurred in May 1905 when Sanger's circus came to town in Bakewell. The *Derby Daily Telegraph* set the stage for the 'exciting scene' that took place during one of the performances:

> The entertainment relies for its attractiveness chiefly upon a performance by three huge elephants, but directly it was sought to make these enter the ring one of the animals was found to be in an exceedingly nasty temper. For a time it stubbornly refused to budge, and when eventually it was induced

The elephant from Lord John Sanger's Circus, which was shot after going on the rampage in Bakewell in 1905. Image reproduced by kind permission of Rod Jewell from his collection. As Rod notes, 'Several different people posed [for postcard photographs] with their guns as if they had shot the elephant!'

to enter the ring it went through its tricks with evident bad grace. Suddenly, to the dismay and alarm of the crowded circus, it turned viciously upon its trainer, and in an instant had felled him to the ground, whereupon it sank upon its knees with the obvious intention of crushing the life out of the unfortunate man's body. Some say the brute deliberately lowered its head and thrust its tusks through the prostrate trainer's thigh.[21]

Reading through this paragraph of the news report 117 years down the line, when a vast majority of the British public now will be opposed to the use of animals such as elephants in a circus act, there are a number of the writer's word choices that leap out at the reader as jarring because of a change in attitude. To most modern eyes, the 'attractiveness' of the entertainment described would be non-existent; how much 'grace' would any of us show if thrust into the limelight and forced to perform in a crowd of strangers were we not in the mood; and who would twenty-first-century readers deem to be the 'brute' of the piece? Yes, the trainer was certainly 'unfortunate' in being publicly crushed by the elephant, but at some point along the line he made a conscious choice to do this for a living, and it could be argued that the incident in Bakewell was simply the natural outcome of a human trying to impose their authority upon a much larger wild animal.

However, whatever the sensibilities of the age, clearly an escaped elephant on the rampage through a market town is a situation that needs bringing under control, so the beast was subsequently rounded up and shot. The *Sheffield Daily Telegraph* of 30 May reported that, 'The carcase of the elephant which caused so much excitement in Bakewell last week has now been removed from the field on which it was shot, and conveyed to a field off the Ashford-road, where a huge grave, from 11ft. to 12ft. in depth, was dug for its reception, and a large quantity of quicklime was placed in the grave for the purpose of hastening decomposition.'[22]

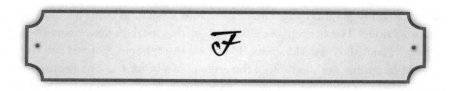

FIRE

Given fire's importance over the centuries in sustaining human life through heating and cooking, it is unsurprising that it should be deeply entwined with ritual belief.

The 'Town and County Gossip' section of the *Derby Daily Telegraph* on Monday, 14 September 1908, offered an intriguing report of a midsummer bonfire that took place near Belper around the mid-nineteenth century:

> The 'Bael-fire' of Whalton, in Northumberland, an account of which was published in the 'Manchester Guardian' last July, is believed at Whalton to be absolutely the last of the Midsummer-eve bonfires that once were common in the North. In Derbyshire the custom certainly lasted on into a time within living memory. A correspondent of 'Notes and Queries' remembers that nearly sixty years ago he saw on Midsummer-night a big bonfire blazing on the highest point of the Chevin, a mile from the right bank of the Derwent, between Belper and Milford. The folks called it 'Belfire', and his mother had seen them ever since she was a little girl. About the fire there were boys and men from the villages and farms near. There was a good bit of horseplay, and drinkings from brown jugs were frequent; but there was no dancing proper, though a good deal of hopping, skipping, and jumping was going on.[23]

As well as the main large bonfire, there was a sort of junior version for the local children:

> 'As certain as the end of June and the beginning of July came,' adds the correspondent, 'we youngsters made little fires for days together, composed of dry keks and grass with sticks and twigs, and, joining hands in a ring, danced round the fires whooping and yelling, the climax being the pulling by one half of the ring of the other half through the fire. Then we all joined in kicking out the fire, scattering the remains in all directions. Who taught us this I do not know.'[24]

Bailey (2019) highlights the origin of the name 'Chevin' as being a Celtic word meaning 'ridge'. The site remains a focal point, one local resident remembering in *Milford and Makeney Milestones*, 'It was on the Chevin that we saw in the New Millennium, huddled round the embers of a bonfire as one century died and another was heralded by fireworks spectacularly exploding on all sides for miles around.'[25]

In the late 1970s, ceremonial bonfires to mark the high points of the old pagan year were still being held around the Longdendale Valley, as Dr Ann Ross noted plummily in her commentary to the *Chronicle* documentary: 'On this dark Derbyshire hillside, on May Day eve, for those who look beyond the street lamps, there are always the tell-tale pinpricks of the Beltane fires. Outsiders are forbidden here.'[26]

Bonfire Night is still widely celebrated on or around 5 November. In Oaker, the small hamlet where I grew up in the 1980s, a local family, the Reagans, who lived in a large Victorian house with a big garden, offered open house for all the other residents to come round, pooling resources of fireworks and bonfire food like parkin and brandy snaps. While the twenty-first century has seen a marked shift away from these kind of communal back garden bonfires towards large, rather sterile, organised displays ('health and safety' culture being an influencing factor here), Thomas Ratcliffe, who grew up at Coxbench, writing in the 1870s, seems premature in his reports of Bonfire Night's demise. He wrote in *Long Ago: A Journal of Popular Antiquities*:

> The Fifth of November, one other of the customs with which our fathers were wont to indulge themselves once a year, is dying out – has been dying out for the last twenty years. Here and there the fun is still kept alive, but the places are few and far between. Twenty years ago, the Fifth of November was looked forward to as an event which must be very much honoured, not by school-boys only, who honour most things after their fashion, but by 'old boys', too.[27]

Ratcliffe's choice of language throughout paints a picture of a very male-centric participation of marking the date. He goes on to provide us with an interesting description of how the day was celebrated in a Derbyshire village[28] in the nineteenth century:

> I have lively remembrances how this custom was enacted in some two or three Derbyshire villages. For weeks previously the youngsters hoarded up

the halfpence, to be when the time came, invested in small brass cannon, powder, squibs, crackers, and whatnot. A few days before the Fifth, the effigy of 'Guy Fox' [*sic*] was made up. Very villainous-looking was he made, the whole resources of boy-art being brought into requisition to effect that end. On the morning of that day, the effigy was carried round the district, seated in, and tied to, a chair; from one hand dangled the traditional lantern. A cart and horse accompanied the guy, when practicable, to carry away the heavy contributions, such as lumps of coal and logs of wood, for every house was solicited to give 'summut to'ard th' bun-fire hole' [something towards the bonfire hole]. It was a general rule for each house to contribute either a few pence or something to burn. If the houses refused to give, whatever was handy, and suitable for the fire, would certainly be taken.[29]

In addition, Ratcliffe supplies a rhyme, which was shouted at every house during the perambulations:

Remember, remember
Th' Fifth of November,
Th' Gunpowder Plot,
Shal ne'er be forgot!
Pray g'is a bit o' coal,
Ter stick I' th' bun-fire hole!
A stick an' a stake,
For King George's sake –
A stowp an' a reel,
Or else wey'll steal![30]

W. Walker recounts a truncated, but similar in essence, rhyme that was recited at Tideswell on 5 November as the children went round the houses there begging for fuel to put on their bonfires:

Coal, coal, a bonfire hole,
A stick and a stake
For King George's sake.
If you please will you give me a penny
For my bonfire hole.[31]

This practice had died out by the time Walker recorded it in 1951.

Another children's Bonfire Night rhyme from Brimington, Chesterfield, was submitted to *Notes and Queries* in 1919 by G.C. Moore Smith of Sheffield:

> Bonfire night!
> The moon shines bright.
> Forty little angels dressed in white.
> Can you eat a biscuit?
> Can you smoke a pipe?
> Can you go a-courting
> At ten o'clock at night?[32]

Joseph M. Severn records a memory of an enhanced Bonfire Night in the village where he grew up in the nineteenth century, Codnor, located in the coalfields of the Amber Valley:

A large bonfire in Chapel-en-le-Frith Market Place, 1930s.

They had the biggest bonfires here [at an area of terraced housing called Daykins Row, described as an 'out-of-the-way secluded cul-de-sac'] on Guy Fawkes nights of any in the locality. As most of the boys' fathers and brothers were pit workers, there was always a plentiful supply of gunpowder, and the laying of long powder trains, the firing of rudely made cannons, the letting off of squibs, the roar and blaze of a great fire, and the roasting of potatoes, made this an outstanding event.[33]

Crichton Porteous relates in *The Ancient Customs of Derbyshire* (1976) that at Chapel-en-le-Frith in the first half of the twentieth century it was the custom of the townspeople to bring material for their large communal bonfire to store in the Market Place in the weeks leading up to the event. In 1935 an unnamed official took umbrage to this practice and ordered the fuel to be removed to the local tip. Undeterred, the locals scoured the area on the morning of 5 November for alternative combustibles including old wooden house beams, and produced an even bigger fire than the one originally intended. The resulting heat split nearby plate glass shop windows. In a less heritage-conscious-age than our own, the bonfire was constructed around the medieval market cross, which caused fire damage to the stonework.

GOITRE, OR 'DERBYSHIRE NECK'

A goitre is a swelling of the thyroid gland that causes a visible lump or enlargement in a person's neck. It is caused by a lack of iodine and was particularly prevalent around the limestone areas of Derbyshire until the 1930s when it declined, hence the nickname.

Waging a one-man campaign against the resurgence of Derbyshire Neck in the first half of the twentieth century was a local doctor with a suitably altruistic name – Dr Goodfellow of Chesterfield. Between July and September 1944, the authorities of landlocked Chesterfield put on a programme of events in the town's Queen's Park as part of the 'Holidays at Home' scheme, which aimed to compensate for the restricted freedom of movement that was still in place due to the ongoing Second World War. There were donkey rides, cricket matches, a horticultural show and amateur dramatics performances, but surely the most bizarre element of the festivities was the hanging of iodine diffusers in the trees of the park by Dr Goodfellow. The good doctor claimed that as a result of his dispensers, there was more iodine in Queen's Park than on Blackpool beach.

A previous scheme of Goodfellow's for warding off goitre in the locality was encouraging the wearing of pottery lockets made by Oldfields round the neck that contained iodine tablets.

GUISING

Up to the early years of the twentieth century, it would have been a common sight around the Christmas and New Year period to see mysterious bands of strangely attired and masked figures roaming the towns and villages of Derbyshire, calling at neighbourhood houses in the hope of being rewarded by a few coins or some festive food and drink.

These were the local guisers, and their performances could either consist of the simple singing of Christmas carols while wearing outrageous costumes, or a more complex enactment of a Hero versus Villain combat play involving the slaying and subsequent bringing back to life of the protagonist.

This was a once-widespread midwinter ritual across Britain, and elsewhere more likely to be known as a 'mummer's play', with the players being termed 'mummers'. However, in Derbyshire the performers tended to be referred to as 'guisers' (from the act of dis-*guise*) – a name also employed in Northumberland and Scotland.

In the early 1980s, spin-off groups from both Winster Morris and Ripley Morris teams formed revival guising groups. There was a historic precedent in both cases: the Ripley team collected the text that formed the basis of their play from 90-year-old Percy Cook, who still remembered all the words from when he last performed it as a youth in the nearby hamlet of Hammersmith back in 1904. At Winster there is a very strong pedigree for this kind of behaviour: a photograph dated to around 1870 when antiquarian, writer, artist and newspaper editor Llewellynn Jewitt was living at Winster Hall, depicting a group of curiously attired characters in the grounds of the Hall, is reckoned to be the oldest-known photograph of mummers or guisers taken anywhere in the world. The current Winster team used this photo as the inspiration behind their costumes and props when they revived in 1980.

Jewitt's diary for 1867 makes it clear that if living at one of the larger houses of the neighbourhood, you could expect several visits from the local guising groups over the Christmas period:

December 26th: This evening we had several sets of children 'guising', dressed up in all sorts of queer ways, and singing one thing or other. The 'Hobby Horse' came too. Five men – one as a devil, one as a woman, one as an old woman with a besom, one with the Hobby Horse, and one as something or other else. We had them in the kitchen and gave them money.

December 27th: Troops of children 'guising' again. We gave something to each lot. In the evening the Winster 'snap Dragon' and 'Hobby Horse' conjoined came to us – ten men, one as Snap Dragon, two with Hobby Horses, two devils, etc., etc. We had them in the kitchen and gave them money.

December 28th: This evening the Wensley 'Mummers' came – nine – and we had them in the kitchen and gave them refreshments and money. They played 'Robin Hood' excellently well, and sang afterwards several excellent songs. They were most interesting. Troops of children again.

December 30th: This evening had two parties of 'guisers' in the house. The first – five – were so dull and stupid that I packed them off soon. The second set – eleven – with 'snap Dragon' and two 'Hobby Horses' were very good, and sang and recited well.[34]

Above left: Winster Guisers performing at Elton Village Hall, December 2017.

Above right: Winster Guisers and their 'horse' performing at a private party in Winster, December 2018.

Above left: A group shot of the Ripley Guisers in 2017.

Above right: A buxom Mick Buckley of the Ripley Guisers makes an entrance during a performance at the Poet & Castle, Codnor, in December 2017.

These entries suggest the quality of the guising performances could vary considerably. Additionally, while many people looked forward to the ramshackle entertainment a visit from the guisers brought and ascribed them as bringing luck for the forthcoming year, they were by no means universally welcome, as the 'Gleanings From the Peak' column in the *Derbyshire Times* of Saturday, 15 December 1883 made clear:

> Several well-known residents of Bakewell are determined to check, if not abolish, the practice of 'guising' as hitherto carried on in the town at Christmas time. 'Guising' as cherished here, is a somewhat peculiar, and doubtless ancient custom, and will not be crushed without some trouble. But there can be no doubt, the householders have the law on their side should their masked and dumb visitors be at all obstinate when ordered to make their exit. 'Guising', although apparently harmless, has some drawbacks, one of which is very serious, as example will show. Last year the residence of a well-known professional gentleman in Bakewell was visited by some of these reminders of Christmas time, and as usual, having gained admission they preferred not to go when requested. The lord of the house, however, being a muscular individual, did not appreciate this defiance, and promptly locked the door and expressed his determination to satisfy himself to the identity of his callers. The guisers refused to unrobe or to unmask, but their entertainer [i.e., the householder] was as strong minded as he was physically powerful, and having invoked the aid of an unmerciful looking stick, he eventually vanquished his visitors. One of the number proved to be a well-known character who had previously, and who has also since that time, been convicted for serious offences. It is neither pleasant nor desirable to have such characters in possession, even in the guise of 'guisers'.[35]

Both the revived Ripley and Winster Guisers groups have commendably raised many thousands of pounds for local charities, and had a good laugh while doing so, in the years that they have been active.

HEN RACING

The first Saturday in August sees crowds descend on Bonsall for an unusual sporting contest, and one with a supposedly historic pedigree around these parts: the annual World Hen Racing Championships, held in the car park of the village's eccentric pub, the Barley Mow. This can quite justifiably call itself a world championship event, having in the past attracted competitors from Australia, Finland, Spain and the USA (although they all borrowed British chickens in order to participate).

The historical origination of hen racing as a local custom is a little sketchy to say the least. We can say for certain that the first supposedly 'revived' race took place at Bonsall in 1992, organised by the Barley Mow's then-landlord Alan Webster. Alan claims rather sketchily in an interview that can be found on YouTube that he 'had heard' hen racing took place 'in the area' 'in the past'.

After Alan retired, new landlords Collette Dewhurst and David Wragg took over and kept the tradition going. Speaking to *Derbyshire Life* in 2013, new landlord Wragg explained: 'We think it started with farmers having a drink outside the pub and watching the chickens scratching about, and saying to each other, "I bet that black hen passes the bucket before the white one".'[36] A 2011 *Derby Telegraph* preview of the event specifically pinpoints the location of the supposed 'historical' hen racing in Ible, a tiny and isolated hamlet consisting of around three farms, eight houses, a lamp post and a cow, 4 miles up the road from Bonsall.

That was reiterated during the racing by landlady Colette, who did a superbly entertaining job of compering proceedings during my visit in 2015, when 7-year-old Jack Allsop-Smith of Ible raced his chickens named 'Plucked It' and 'Cooked It'. However, Colette stated that the racing took place in 'medieval' times, contradicting the official event T-shirts that could be seen on sale on the stall just behind her, which proclaimed 'Established 1892' (a suspiciously neat 100 years before the 'revival').

Let us delve a little deeper into the supposed pedigree of hen racing as a supposed traditional Derbyshire sport.

Above left: A hen crosses the finishing line at Bonsall Hen Races, 2015.

Above right: Participants and their owners at Bonsall Hen Races in 2015, including Major Matt Beech on his stag do (on the left, in chicken costume).

Further research has led me to concede that perhaps there is indeed something more concrete to the concept of chicken racing as a sport in the area. An extract from Jim Drury's highly entertaining series of reminiscences of village life, *'Fetch The Juicy Jam!' and other Memories of Birchover*, further suggests that the idea of chicken racing has been a common leg pull around these parts for a good while:

Work on the Bakewell Rural District water scheme started in 1954 with The Green in Birchover as the depot for the area. The contractors were a Manchester-based company called O. R. M. A. C.. Two Irishmen were the owners, O'Riley and MacCluggan. Some travelled by the company bus each day from Manchester; others sought lodgings in the village. [...]

The Irishman's love of horse racing and gambling is well known but one night in the Red Lion some of them were taken for a ride by old Phillip. The conversation went something like this,

'Where you working at now?' asked Phillip.

'Up at Aldwark,' came the reply.

'Oh aye, it'll soon be Aldwark Hen Races won't it?'

A look of amazement spread over the Irish faces and one of them said, 'Indeed to God, I never heard of hen races before. I'd sure like to see them. When is it held?'

'On th'Tuesday before the first snow,' said Phillip, without even the faintest smile.

'Begorra, I wouldn't want to be at Aldwark if it's going to snow, much as I'd like to see the hen racing!'[37]

Aldwark is a tiny and isolated upland village between Matlock and Ashbourne with a population that has remained steady at around forty inhabitants in censuses over the past 100 years.

I encountered some further apparent photographic evidence reproduced on page 65 of the late Winster local historian and postcard collector Michael Greatorex's local history book *Winster – People and Places in Postcards*. Here we find an apparently genuine photo from the 1920s or '30s believed to be of Winster resident Ben Brassington seemingly taken at the 'Aldwark Hen Races'. The tall form of Brassington stands dressed in rustic attire holding a wooden cane with a wicker basket strewn around his neck in which are contained at least two white fowl. A young boy (who for some reason appears to have a blackened face) holds a slate with 'Aldwark Hen Races' chalked on it and also a piece of rope that seems to be tied around Brassington's hand. Both figures are stood in a field and in the background can be seen a typical Derbyshire dry stone wall.

I uncovered a further historic reference to hen racing in a *Derbyshire Times* report on the Elton Carnival from 7 July 1928, where, tucked away among a long list of prize-winners at the festivities, the second prize winner in the 'Gent's comic' category is given as 'hen races, Mr. Boam, Winster'. Could the person depicted in the photo in Greatorex's collection actually be Mr Boam, at Elton? When I made contact with Michael, who passed away in 2019, about the photo in his collection, he replied, 'My tenuous link to Ben Brassington was because the photo was supplied to me by Ben's son, Eric, who is still alive living in Cumbria and he speculated that it was his Dad. […] Mr Boam, Winster, doesn't help us much as there would be numerous Mr Boams in Winster during the late 1920s.'

As well as Aldwark, another epicentre of the sport of hen racing appears to be the aforementioned Ible, a similarly remote spot whose only other claim to fame is as the setting of the short story by D.H. Lawrence, 'Wintry Peacock'. Lawrence and his German wife Frieda lived at Mountain Cottage just outside Middleton-by-Wirksworth, having been turfed out of their Cornish cottage near Zennor, accused of spying for the Germans during the febrile atmosphere of the First World War. In exile, the pair relocated to the similarly remote Mountain Cottage, which, as its name suggests, clings to the steep hillside above the wild Via Gellia road in the valley bottom below. The Lawrences could see Ible across the other side of the valley and Lawrence used to walk over there often. Many of Lawrence's works of fiction have a heavy basis in fact and 'Wintry Peacock', whose narrative revolves around a local farmer's wife who receives a letter intimating that her husband, who is away in Europe during the First World War, has in fact been doing more than just fighting out there and has fathered a child by a French woman. It is believed that this version of events had a heavy basis in actual events that happened to a real-life couple during Lawrence's stay; however, he cunningly covered his tracks by changing the name of the hamlet in the fictional story – to 'Tible'!

In response to a comment mentioning Ible Hen Races on the 'Old Matlock pics' Facebook group, Rob Rouse remembered: 'My dad used to say that when I was a nipper. "Dad where's Mum?" "She's gone to the hen races at Ible!"'

A key piece of evidence on the trail of the sport of hen racing is a televised item broadcast by ITV's *Central News East* in 1986, which can be viewed on the website of MACE (the Media Archive for Central England). The piece, presented by Phil Bayles, purports to be an expose into the world of the 'Wirksworth and Ible Hen Racing'. The report begins with establishing shots of Wirksworth market and the transit of chickens in large wicker baskets. The feature is apparently prompted by animal rights protesters complaining about the treatment of chickens during the races, which are reported as taking place monthly. A Rolls-Royce is shown that belongs to professional gambler 'Big H', who places large bets on the racing. 'Under the pretext that we were recording a feature on Wirksworth market', the cameras move inside the Hope and Anchor pub, where some picturesque country folk are seen handling chickens. Some of these people sport hi-vis jackets and badges that identify the wearer as a 'steward' or a 'starter'. Attempts at initiating an interview lead to patrons fleeing the pub with their flat caps pulled down over their heads, and when questioning the landlord Bayles is told to 'sod off'. Rule sheets for the racing are shown on camera that decree 'Bumping, pecking, treading or flapping warrants instant disqualification'; 'Finger starts are considered very ungentlemanly and can result in a considerable fine for the stable and life ban for the handler'; 'Feather painting and the practice of slipping a "ringer", which has been known in the past, is considered a serious breach of conduct. Consequently, a very close inspection by the stewards is now adopted'; 'Night races have been known, indoor races in

Archive photo from the 1920s believed to show Winster resident Ben Brassington, seemingly at 'Aldwark Hen Races'. Image reproduced by kind permission of the late Michael Greatorex, from the Eric Brassington collection.

bad conditions, 3' hurdles are used in indoor events'; and 'stewards are appointed in secret to officiate on particular racing days'. A racing form book with odds (giving a race location as Elton) and a poster on the wall for 'The Duke's Challenge Cup' are also filmed. The film crew then move on to a 'secret location' to film a race. 'It's a very old tradition, it's gone on since 1832,' claims one entrant while stroking his chicken. 'Some of these Animal Rights people, they do think it's cruel, and it has been kept a little bit under cover, but there's nothing wrong with it at all.' The chickens are shown about to be released from starting traps made out of wood and chicken wire, before the camera crew are rumbled and chased away by the landowner. So, conclusive proof of hen racing as a traditional Derbyshire custom with a historic pedigree? Well, it might be worth taking note of the transmission date the story went out on the local news – 1 April 1986 …

As with the spoof local news item, the races held on the first Saturday of August at Bonsall are run subject to certain rules. These state that once owners have released their chickens onto the track, no further contact is permitted. However, a collaborator stationed beyond the finishing line is allowed to encourage the chickens towards them using any method that they see fit – on my most recent visit this included shouting, 'Chuck, chuck'; shaking a metal pan containing chicken feed or a plastic tub of mealworms; offering a bucket of spinach while blowing a whistle; and brandishing a spade (a Pavlovian tactic – apparently the chicken whom this particular technique was directed towards associates the spade with gardening and the turning over of earth, which lures worms to the surface for it to eat).

A new innovation at 2015's hen racing event was the introduction of a finishing line camera for any steward's enquiries, which was invigilated by tuxedoed Barley Mow regular (and serial letter writer to the broadsheets) Victor Launert, who was constantly hunched over a laptop (protected from the intermittent rain showers by an umbrella placed over it) studying the footage.

This, Victor explains with a note of sadness for more carefree days of yore, marks 'the professionalisation of hen racing'.

Each year there is often some sort of interlude at Bonsall to break up the racing. On my first visit to the races back in 2003, with the popularity at the time of the BBC's *Robot Wars* TV show, there was a robotic chicken race, with two remote-controlled model chickens competing. On my return visit in 2015, there was a contest staged between two competitors who had to pluck eggs from a bucket and smack them down onto their forehead; the majority were hard-boiled but some were not and doused the combatants with yolk and albumen – essentially, a form of eggy Russian Roulette. One of the entrants for this was Major Matt Beech, who found himself at the hen races by surprise as part of his stag do organised by his colleagues in the forces, who had dressed him in a chicken outfit consisting of red fright wig, yellow tights, rubber talons, paisley Y-fronts and multi-coloured feathers stuck down his arms.

So having mulled over all this evidence, is hen racing a genuine Derbyshire tradition, or merely one gigantic leg pull to bring in business to the Barley Mow? Despite many hours of dedicated research, I'm still personally none the wiser, so you'll just have to turn up at Bonsall on the first Saturday in August and decide for yourself.

Interestingly, the tradition appears to be one that is spreading across Derbyshire. Great Hucklow, as part of its Wakes Week and Well Dressing Festivities in August, has staged a 'Chicken Run' race in recent years (other exciting events on offer throughout the week included a buggy race and a 'Potato Race weigh-in' to establish the biggest potato grown in the village that year).

I made a fieldwork trip to Great Hucklow in 2016 to witness their hen races. A poster informed me that the 2016 event I was attending was the fourth annual Great Hucklow Chicken Run. A grass roadside verge had been cordoned off with plastic fencing, and four ornamental chickens and a cockerel were fenced in ready to race.

Hen racing, Great Hucklow style. Chicken run event at Great Hucklow, Wakes, 2016.

The form was a little different to Bonsall – for starters, in Great Hucklow bets were taken on which chicken would win, and guesses made as to what time the winning chicken would complete the course (with the money going to Great Hucklow Community Spirit, and prizes issued to those who got the closest guess to the race time; in the first heat a Cadbury's chocolate bar was awarded to a delighted lady from Grindleford for being a second off the winning time of fifty-six seconds). A printed sheet of paper listed the Hucklow racing rules:

- £1 per 'time guess', per chicken, per run – for all runs
- As many guesses as you like allowed per run PLEASE!
- Only official chicken coaxer allowed on the track during the run
- No 'fowl play', unofficial use of mealy [*sic*] worms or corn allowed by the crowd
- All winners will receive a prize

Racing consisted of four heats. As the theme for that year's Wakes Week was the 150th anniversary of the birth of Beatrix Potter, the hens had all been renamed in reference to Potter characters: Chicken Peter Rabbit, Chicken Squirrel Nutkin, Chicken Jeremy Fisher, Chicken Jemima Puddle Duck, and Chicken Mrs Tiggywinkle, although I overhead one lady saying that the real names of two of her chickens that were in the running were Gilbert and George, after the performance art duo with a penchant for nudity and bodily functions. As per the rules, one difference to Bonsall was that at the starting end of the course, one lady (presumably the 'official chicken coaxer') shepherded the hens towards the finishing line, while at the other another lady threw down pellets of 'Hentastic Smart Start' chicken feed to encourage the fowl onwards.

Kirk Ireton also mount competitive hen racing as part of their Wakes Week, with the 'Golden Cluck' contest seeing hens racing down the village main street.

J

ILKESTON CHARTER FAIR

Ilkeston can be found in the Erewash Valley district of Derbyshire, 2 miles from the boundary of the city of Nottingham. Despite being somewhat overshadowed by the famous Goose Fair that takes place annually in Nottingham, Ilkeston has its own annual Charter Fair, which is actually older than Nottingham's. Ilkeston's fair charter was first granted by King Henry III in 1252, giving it a whole thirty-two years' extra pedigree to the Goose Fair, which was inaugurated in 1284.

In addition, the Goose Fair outgrew its original central site in Nottingham's market square and in 1928 was moved out to a site on the outskirts of the city at the Forest Recreation Ground; Ilkeston's fair still takes place in and around the town's market square and the surrounding streets.

In practice, being so close to the Goose Fair – both geographically, and with the two events being held close together in October – has probably ultimately proved beneficial to Ilkeston's fair and helped it to continue to thrive. I visited both fairs in 2019, and recognised many of the same rides and stalls at each. Both fairs had food stalls selling traditional delicacies associated with the two events: hot mushy peas with mint sauce and packets of brandy snaps and Grantham gingerbread.

Originally, Ilkeston's fair took place in mid-August on the feast day of the Assumption of the Blessed Virgin of Our Lady. The town also held an annual 'Mop Fair', or hiring fair, every October, where agricultural workers put themselves on public parade to be picked out and taken on by local employers for the tenure of the forthcoming farming year. In 1888, both fairs were amalgamated, to be held during the town's October Wakes Week. It remains one of the oldest and largest street fairs in the whole of Europe. The traditional date for the opening of Ilkeston's Charter Fair now follows something of a complex formula, being held on the first Thursday after the first Sunday after 11 October (got that?).

The fair is well supported by the local authorities, who maintain their ancient tradition with a sense of pride. In 1931 an official opening ceremony for the fair was introduced, which takes place on the forecourt of the Town

Local council dignitaries take a spin on the Ferris wheel at the opening of Ilkeston Charter Fair in 2019.

Mayor of Erewash Sue Beardsley and colleagues road testing the dodgems at Ilkeston Charter Fair in 2019.

Hall. That year the then-Mayor of Ilkeston, Councillor Beardsley, became the first mayor to inaugurate the fair in this fashion by ringing a pair of bells at midday following the proclamation of the public reading of the fair charter.

After the ringing of the bells, the assembled gold-chain-clad dignitaries (all councillors and mayors from the surrounding area and their plus ones dressed in their finest outfits) then step across the forecourt to road test the rides, beginning with a spin on the big wheel, from which elevated vantage point they can gain a good bird's-eye view of the festivities. Next they proceed en masse for a ride on the dodgems (presumably this exercise provides a good opportunity for the participants to work off some of the pent-up disagreements and rivalries that have built up in the council debating chamber over the preceding twelve months), before sampling the horrors of the ghost train and the more traditional cake walk ride.

One phenomenon that has fallen by the wayside over the years as the twentieth century has progressed and public tastes have changed are the various fairground sideshows or 'freak shows'. A regular attraction to be seen at the Ilkeston fairs of the nineteenth century was the home-grown spectacle of Samuel Taylor, the 'Ilkeston Giant', who measured in at a remarkable 7ft 4½in tall. Taylor fell into the fairground world by accident, having visited a travelling fair at nearby Castle Donington as a 16-year-old in 1832. Upon entering the sideshow tent as a punter, when the curtain was pulled back to reveal the fair's resident giant it transpired he measured about a foot less than Taylor; all the audience's eyes were on Samuel rather than the man on stage, who subsequently physically attacked Samuel for stealing his thunder. In the brutal world of showbusiness, the ultimate outcome was that the original giant was sacked and Samuel taken on in his place. Taylor later left Ilkeston, becoming the landlord of a pub in Manchester, but retained a great fondness for the town of his upbringing, and would return annually to appear as an attraction at the fair. Following his death in 1875 at the age of 59, Taylor's body was returned to Ilkeston in a huge coffin and met at the train station by the local brass band. His grave alongside a wooden statue of him can be seen in the town's Stanton Road Cemetery.

JUGHOLE CAVE

Jughole Cave, located on Masson Hill, an isolated spot of the White Peak countryside between the villages of Snitterton and Bonsall, retains an eerie air into the twenty-first century. Chill winds emanate from this cavernous gap in the hillside on even the sunniest of summer days and to this day it does not take much of a stretch of the imagination to picture the cave mouth as some sort of portal to the underworld; it is therefore not a surprise to discover that local legends have developed concerning this spot.

In Ernest Paulson's telling of the tale of the Matlock Dragon, it is here at the Jughole Cave that the beast retreats having been defeated (see Dragons), from where his presence causes specific local geological phenomena to occur.

The Jughole Cave was not only home to a resident dragon, but also the ghost of a mad dog, according to the report of Frank H. Brindley, freelance photographer and member of the British Spelcologists Association, which appeared in the *Nottingham Guardian* of 6 June 1953. Brindley had been exploring the Jughole caverns with a party of fellow cavers when he first heard the apparent sound of a dog barking from within the cave system. The party's initial reading of the situation was that someone had cruelly deposited an unwanted dog down one of the many deep shafts into the White Peak countryside that remained from the heyday of lead mining (a couple of decades later in the 1970s, a concerted programme of capping off these dangerous shafts was undertaken after a series of mishaps involving unsuspecting tourists to the area tumbling down them). At the time of the Brindley group's visit there was snow on the ground, so they inspected the surface of the hillside for telltale footprints leading to a shaft but could find none.

The action in Brindley's telling then moved on to the cavers' lodgings for the night: 'Back in Matlock at our hotel, we remarked about the cruelty of someone throwing a dog down an old mine shaft near to where we had explored an old mine. One of our party – a real dog lover, offered a reward to anyone who could give him the name of the person, as we sat in the public bar.'[38]

The entrance to Jughole Cave near Snitterton – home to a dragon and a 'mad dog'.

A conveniently placed elderly local overheard this exchange, then stood up to offer the party some information as to what they may have just experienced: 'I am an old lead miner's son. Do you know what you heard in the Jug-hole caves stopped my father over 80 years ago from mining there. That dog has been known to be in the caverns there for over 200 years.' He went on: 'What you heard was not a live dog, but the ghost of one! You could never get any miners to work there, and rich mines are known to be near it, yet that is why the minerals were never got.'[39]

So far, so *Scooby Doo*. Taking the legend-spouting rustic's words as something of a challenge, Frank and his merry band of meddling speleologists decided to pay a return visit to the Jughole Cave to investigate the mystery of the Mad Ghost Dog further.

Regrettably, with the passing of time, enthusiasm for the scheme waned somewhat: 'A "Meet" was arranged, but unfortunately only two of us turned up. The weather being very wet, with sleet and snow, which as it was at night, most members preferred a warm bed. Stripping under a shelving rock, we changed into shorts, hard hats and climbing boots, and we were complete with lamps and rope, carrying bundle of tallow candles as spares should our lamps fail. Waterproof matches completed the equipment. We crept into the unknown.'[40]

I bet you are on the edge of your seats here, aren't you?

Brindley and his unnamed partner who also eschewed the warmth of their bed to go probing around the Jughole first encountered an 18ft, circular, bell-shaped chamber with an opening in the floor that was 'round, and all glazed with fire [...] proof that Masson Hill is an extinct volcano'. Well, either that, or proof that the local dragon did indeed take shelter here as Ernest Paulson claimed.

Penetrating the fire-glazed opening, the pair discovered another cave below 'which was like an enlarged sponge. Openings on every side, and all dangerous to enter.'[41]

Despite this, the pair gamely entered one of the openings, descending through 60ft of steep tunnel, along which ran an underground river. They emerged into another underground chamber 'beautifully decorated with white crystal rock and festoons of stalactites hanging from every part of the roof'.[42] It was having entered the neighbouring chamber with the river running through it that Brindley and his companion experienced what they had come back for: 'Away in the far distance, somewhere along this river tunnel, we heard the sound of a dog barking, which seemed to end with one long drawn out howl.'[43] Following the source of the sound, they found it changed the closer they got to it: 'Listening again, the dog sound seemed to have changed to many separate barks, finishing with long drawn out howls, which we could not explain.'[44]

Emerging into yet another underground chamber within the Jughole Cave system, Brindley observed that the river they had been following appeared to terminate in a large underground lake. The pair sat on the shore of the lake to rest and ponder their next move. 'We had not sat down more than 10 minutes,' Brindley recounted, 'when across the lake we saw a movement in the water. It appeared to be of some large fish or prehistoric reptile rising out of the depth of the lake and we fully expected to see its gigantic head break water, and give us all a look over. The movement seemed to be some enormous tail turning round in the lake as if to get a nearer view of us, and, fascinated, we waited.'[45]

Could this be some sort of Loch-Ness-style water monster also dwelling underground within the Jughole Caves to complement the Dragon and ghostly Mad Dog? The denouement of Brindley's account turns out to be more prosaic: 'Instead, from the deep lake sounds of a great explosion, followed by other similar crashes, then without any more warning the whole lake began to boil in a most alarming manner. All the water rushed round in a circle, then with an even greater bang, we heard far down in the depth a choking sound, followed by the water suddenly rushing down into the opening of a large funnel-like pipe. Inside a few minutes, all the water had gone, leaving an empty chamber. The only water left was the stream running in and this fell in as a waterfall into the top of the funnel opening. [...] The funnel was one great rock syphon. The explosions of confined air trapped in the bend of the rock syphon were like a dog barking. That was what made the sound which, in the distance, seemed like a dog in pain.'[46]

Mystery solved!

KENNY, BETTY

In Shining Cliff Woods near Ambergate can be found an ancient yew tree that is known as 'Betty Kenny's Tree'. 'Betty' (whose real name was Kate Kenyon) and her husband Luke were employed as charcoal burners and lived within the woods in the 1700s. They constructed their makeshift home with a turf roof around the tree trunk. Within this improvised living space they raised their eight children, rocking the babies to sleep inside a hollowed-out bough of the yew. It has been postulated that the Kenyons left their mark on popular culture: their circumstances are said to be the basis for the well-known nursery rhyme, 'Rock a Bye Baby on the Tree Top'.

Shining Cliff Woods were owned by the Hurt family of Alderwasley Hall, who exhibited a fondness for their unusual tenants. Francis Hurt (1781–1854) commissioned the Royal Academy painter James Ward to produce a painting of Betty and Luke and arranged for them to pose within the dining room of the hall. The painting was exhibited at the Royal Academy in 1814 before being hung in the hall.

Despite their humble living arrangements, the Kenyons lived to a ripe age, with Luke's burial at 96 years of age being recorded in the Wirksworth Parish Registers as taking place on 5 January 1814. Betty, who was 94 at the time of her husband's death, is said to have lived on long enough to dance at a party at the hall held in honour of her 100th birthday.

The yew the family inhabited still stands, although is now a shadow of its former self, having been set alight by vandals in the 1930s. After the Hurt family ceased to live at the Hall in the 1930s, Ward's painting went missing and its current whereabouts are unknown.

KISSING BUNCH, VIOLENCE PROVOKED BY

Come December, the majority of Derbyshire households erect and decorate a Christmas tree – whether that be a freshly cut evergreen, or a plastic replica annually retrieved from storage in the loft. But a once-traditional decoration that was formerly a common sight in the cottages of Derbyshire each yuletide is nowadays very rarely seen: the kissing bunch.

A detailed Victorian description of a kissing bunch sighting from Derbyshire ran as follows:

> The 'kissing bunch' is always an elaborate affair. The size depends on the couple of hoops – one thrust through the other – which forms its skeleton. Each of the ribs is garlanded with holly, ivy, and sprigs of other greens, with bits of coloured ribbons and paper roses, rosy-cheeked apples, specially reserved for this occasion, and oranges. Three small dolls are also prepared, often with much taste, and these represent our Saviour, the mother of Jesus, and Joseph. These dolls generally hang within the kissing bunch by strings from the top, and are surrounded by apples, oranges tied to strings, and various brightly coloured ornaments. Occasionally, however, the dolls are arranged in the kissing bunch to represent a manger-scene … Mistletoe is not very plentiful in Derbyshire; but, generally, a bit is obtainable, and this is carefully tied to the bottom of the kissing bunch, which is then hung in the middle of the house-place, the centre of attention during Christmastide.[47]

Hilda Shepherd (nee Worthy), who grew up in the village of Holloway near Matlock, described the kissing bunch that was produced in her household in correspondence with folklorist Dave Bathe:

> We used to have at Christmas a kissing bunch – two wooden hoops intertwined, and mother would cover them with green and red paper, then would place holly etc. all round. And there was a wood at the back of the house, and we were able to get as much lovely greenery as we wanted, lots of this went round the kissing bunch. Then mother would hang the same baubles on like those on the Christmas tree. Everybody was kissed under the kissing bunch, even Mr Hawkins the milkman.[48]

While combing through old copies of local newspapers for references to the kissing bunch, I came across a surprising item in the 'Police Intelligence' section of the *Derbyshire Times* reporting on a kissing-bunch-related incident that had got out of hand. The piece, 'Cost of a Kiss at Troway',[49] detailed how at this location on the Derbyshire–Sheffield border a certain Joseph Havenhand had ended up in the courtroom as a result of his behaviour towards a Miss Maria Davenport. On the evening of 2 January 1871, following a pleasant time spent with friends at a tea followed by dancing, the prosecutrix went on to a (rather belated) Christmas party where she found herself underneath a kissing bunch being pestered by the forceful Havenhand, who refused to take 'no' for an answer.

Against the backdrop of an ongoing discussion in the early twenty-first century regarding the violence that women face in their day-to-day lives, it is a little jarring to read the newspaper commenting that, 'The case created great amusement in court'; the judge, however, seems more in step with our own times, stating that he was 'of opinion that a young lady should not be kissed, even at Christmas, against her will', and ordering the defendant to pay 12s expenses for his ungentlemanly behaviour.

It would be nice to think that in cottages in the remoter corners of Derbyshire there may be some diehard traditionalists who still produce a kissing bunch for Christmas each year, but for a guaranteed sighting you can head to Revolution House at Whittington Moor, now a suburb of Chesterfield. This unassuming building, maintained by Chesterfield Museums, is a site of national significance – back in 1688 the premises were an alehouse on the edge of remote moorland called the Cock and Pynot (a dialect word for magpie; the two birds now bear Chesterfield's coat of arms in the town crest), and it was within the walls of this building that three noblemen met and plotted a coup leading to the overthrow of King James II. Every December the museum staff decorate the interior in seventeenth-century fashion for Christmas, including a kissing bunch suspended from the beams.

Traditional kissing bunch on display at Revolution House, Chesterfield.

LEAD MINING, POETRY OF MINE NAMES

The Derbyshire landscape has been plundered for its mineral riches since possibly Prehistoric, and certainly Roman, times. In the eighteenth century the antiquarian William Stukeley (1687–1785) issued a warning to anyone considering travelling through Derbyshire: 'Now you pass over barren moors in a perpetual danger of slipping into coalpits and leadmines,'[50] while Sherlock Holmes author Sir Arthur Conan Doyle wrote of the limestone lead mining area of the White Peak in his short story 'The Terror of Blue John Gap', 'All this country is hollow. Could you strike it with some gigantic hammer it would boom like a drum.'

Lead mining was subject to a complex system of laws and rules that were administered by the annual Barmote Courts, which still sit annually in April at The Moot Hall, Wirksworth, albeit nowadays in a largely ceremonial capacity given the extent to which the industry has dwindled since the mid-twentieth century.

Miners were guaranteed a route to wherever lead could be found, and some of these miners' paths still exist as public footpaths criss-crossing the Derbyshire countryside to this day.

Once a prospecting lead miner located a prosperous vein they would give it a distinctive name to mark it out as their territory. These names, along with those given to soughs (channels driven to take water out of the mines), often have a strange poetry of their own:

Hang-worm Mine, Salad Hole, Beans and Bacon Mine, Warm Bath, Old Ladywash, Cackle-Mackle, Wham Rake, Crashpurse Mine, Black Sticking Vein, Luck-in-a-bag, Godbehere Vein, Old Ranter, Windyway Vein, Lousey Level, Dirty Face Shaft, Noger Hole, Raddle-pits, Odin Mine (also known as 'Gank Mouth'), Merlin Mine, Mule Spinner, Frog Hole, Slitherstones, Wanton Legs, Tear Breeches Mine, Blobber Mine, Ringing Rake, Moletrap Rake, Cod Beat, Fiery Dragon, Burning Drake, Old Eye, Ball Eye, Dragon

Above: The sitting of the ceremonial Great Barmote Court at the Moot Hall, Wirksworth, which has regulated lead mining laws in the Peak for over 800 years.

Left: 'T' Owd Man' – Anglo-Saxon carving of a lead miner figure that is thought to be the oldest image of a miner in the world. Originating from Bonsall, he was taken to St Mary's Church, Wirksworth, in about 1870 and installed there.

Eye Vein, Whale Vein, Yule Cheese Level, Ratchwood & Rantor Mines, Have-at-a-venture/Haveadventure Vein, Hab-Nab Vein, Windy Arbour Vein, Cathole Rake, Danger Level, Conqueror Shaft, Dragon Shaft, Drave Vein, Gentlewoman's Vein, Goodluck Mine, Cow Hole, Dungeon Dale Pipe, Raddish Pipe, Crotie Water Pipe, Sweetbottoms Mine and perhaps my own personal favourite, Grey Mare Arse Mine (as well as the similarly dubbed Horsebuttock Vein).

Other mine names reflect the rural nature of the area, and the wildlife that would have surrounded the miners on their journeys to work: Merry Bird, Dunnock Holes Vein, Pienetnest Mine (a pienet or pynot being a local folk dialect name for a magpie), Birds Nest Vein, Magpie Scrins, Ousel Mine, Owlet Hole, Jackdaw Vein, Foxhole Rake, Wren Park.

Tunnels driven under the environs of the village of Wensley to reach lead ore are named 'Gnasher Crawl' and 'Thrutchers Paradise' – both of which would make excellent names for 1970s prog rock bands. As would 'Jacob's Dream Mine', located close to the Via Gellia. Along with the similarly named Stafford's Dream Mine, these names suggest to us that the locations of the lead veins may have been revealed to miners as they slept and, upon waking, they followed up on the information that was cosmically conveyed to them via their slumbering unconscious mind.

LOCATION, LOCATION, LOCATION

Given that Derbyshire is famed for its stunning scenery, it is no surprise that film crews regularly descend on the area to use the county as a backdrop for their productions. One of the earliest Derbyshire-shot films that has survived to this day in the collection of MACE (Media Archive for Central England) is the slightly underwhelming-sounding *Train Arriving at Ilkeston Station*, made in 1900 by the pioneering Edwardian filmmaking duo of Mitchell and Kenyon.

By the following decade, the grammar of film had developed to the point where filmmakers felt able to tackle slightly more ambitious subject matter than trains arriving in stations. *The Mountaineer's Romance*, from 1912, directed by Charles Raymond, very deliberately featured the dramatic Peakland scenery of Dovedale as a backdrop to the melodramatic interplay between the four main characters: Nan, the Mountaineer's Sister; Ben, Her Brother; Jim, Her Sweetheart; and Myrtle, The Cause Of All The Trouble. 'This Photo-Play was enacted around the beautiful Peak District, Derbyshire,' the wobbly title card announces at the beginning of the film, demonstrating that this part of the country had come to be lodged in the popular consciousness as such several decades prior to the Peak District National Park being formally inaugurated as the UK's first national park in 1951. The siblings Nan and Ben are played by real-life husband and wife duo H.O. (Oceano Henry Oscar) Martinek and Ivy Martinek, who had both previously been circus performers with Barnum and Bailey.

The Peveril of the Peak Hotel at Dovedale receives a healthy dose of free publicity in a plot-advancing shot of a letter written on the hotel's headed notepaper requesting that Ben and Jim call at the hotel the following morning to guide a party of visiting Americans through the Peaks.

We know that Myrtle, one member of this group of Yanks, is going to be trouble (her introductory title card rather gives the game away), and the film's central conflict arises when Nan snoops at Myrtle's mountain-based antics through binoculars and observes her friskily hugging and kissing Jim at the culmination of the ramble. Somehow equating this to mean that Jim is conducting an affair with this woman (who he only met that morning, and has only ever spent time in company with halfway up a mountain accompanied by a party of rambling Americans), she sets her enraged brother Ben on him. Ben, who clearly possesses something of a quick temper, finds the unsuspecting Jim relaxing halfway up a Dovedale mountain and promptly launches into a frenzied knife attack on him; in the ensuing melee Jim falls into the River Dove below, which sweeps him away. Luckily the siblings' error is realised in time and Ben consequently rescues Jim from the water; they are next shown smoking their pipes up a mountain and laughing convivially with Nan. 'All's Well That Ends Well', as the final title card has it, wrapping matters up neatly.

While he was born and bred in the neighbouring county of Nottinghamshire, like many Notts folk the author D.H. Lawrence enjoyed regular sojourns across the border into Derbyshire. His sister Ada recounted with fondness after his death an Easter ramble led by Lawrence from Alfreton train station to the ruined manor of South Wingfield, Crich Stand and Whatstandwell.[51] As has been previously mentioned, the itinerant author and his German wife Frieda spent a spell living in Derbyshire in 1918–19 (*see* Hen Racing).

Lawrence's texts have long been associated with a sense of taboo-busting raunchiness (his fellow Eastwood natives were reputedly ambivalent about having produced a literary genius; he is said to have been referred to in the town of his birth as 'that mucky man'). Therefore, with the rapid new era of permissiveness the late 1960s ushered in and the consequent relaxation of film censorship rules, Lawrence's 'mucky' texts became prime source material for film adaptations – and an excuse to get top-grade stars to get their kit off in front of the cameras under the veneer of literary respectability.

Lawrence frequently used a mixture of actual and fictionalised ('Woodlinkin', 'Bonsall Head') Derbyshire locations throughout his novels, so it was a natural development that the 1960s film crews adapting his work should decamp to Derbyshire. Ken Russell's 1969 adaptation of *Women in Love*, most famous for its ground-breaking naked wrestling scene between Oliver Reed and Allestree's own Alan Bates, featured several scenes shot in Derbyshire. These include a wedding filmed at St Giles Church, Matlock, with a semi-detached Victorian villa on New Street in the same town representing the exterior of the Brangwen sisters' home. Further south in the county, the Elvaston Castle Country Park is used for a lakeside party on the Crich estate, with Kedleston Hall, Derby war memorial and Belper also featuring.

The following year, 1970, saw the release of *The Virgin and the Gypsy*, an adaptation of a lesser-known Lawrence novella. Again the cameras were rolling in Derbyshire, with Youlgrave and Raper Lodge just outside the village, Cromford Railway Station, Beeley Moor, Matlock and Derwent Dam all making appearances on the silver screen. Many Youlgrave residents of the time were coaxed into period costume as extras.

In the early 1970s a Spanish–Italian film crew helmed by director Jorge Grau rolled up in Derbyshire to shoot exterior scenes for the zombie film *The Living Dead at the Manchester Morgue* (also known under the title *Let Sleeping Corpses Lie*). Following a chance encounter between Edna (Cristina Galbó) and George (Ray Lovelock), the pair find themselves out in the English countryside together, where the Ministry of Agriculture is testing a new experimental machine designed to kill insects using ultra-sonic radiation. Unfortunately this new technology has one very serious unforeseen side effect – it reanimates the dead and turns them into murderous zombies. Whoops!

Derbyshire locations that made the final cut of the movie include the famous stepping stones across the River Dove at Dovedale; Castleton (doubling as the fictional 'Southgate' of the film – the dramatic gorge of Winnats Pass features, as does The Castle pub, here renamed 'The Old Owl Hotel', an ever-so-slightly creepy establishment where the protagonists check in for the night, complete with real-life sleepy owl on a perch hanging from the ceiling of the hotel's reception); and Hathersage churchyard (in whose grounds can be found the supposed grave of Little John, Robin Hood's comrade). However, for some reason, within the narrative of the film the landscape that the characters are blundering about in is made out to be another national park close to the titular city of Manchester – the Lake District.

Derbyshire usually gets lumped in with the East Midlands region, but the reality is more nuanced, with the county feeling in practice more like a kind of borderland between the Midlands and northern England – personally, the north to me feels like it begins somewhere in the vicinity of Wirksworth, where the surrounding scenery as you enter the White Peak becomes bleaker and hillier (by comparison with the flatter and more pastoral rural landscapes of south Derbyshire) and Northern dialect begins to enter the lingo: gennel, mardy. Travel onwards and upwards into north-west Derbyshire and this unquestionably feels like the north of England: by the time you reach the area around Glossop, a Mancunian twang has begun to enter the local accent.

The League of Gentlemen comedy troupe comprises Steve Pemberton, Reece Shearsmith and Mark Gatiss – three northerners who met as students at Bretton Hall drama school – alongside non-acting writing partner Jeremy Dyson. Between them the group devised a character-based comedy series revolving around a characteristically northern small town peopled by eccentric oddballs. In their BBC Radio 4 series the fictional town in question is named 'Spent', but when the team transferred *The League of Gentlemen* to BBC2 it was rechristened Royston Vasey (the real name of the comedian Roy 'Chubby' Brown, who makes a recurring cameo appearance in the second series as the town's foul-mouthed mayor). The production team initially struggled to find a suitable small and quintessentially northern town for filming to represent Royston Vasey, before discovering Hadfield in north-west Derbyshire. The majority of the series was filmed in and around the town, however exterior shots of the iconic 'Local Shop' owned by villainous shopkeepers Tubbs and Edward were shot on Marsden Moor, 15 miles to the north and over the boundary in West Yorkshire.

Despite the undercurrent of bleak horror that runs through the show's humour, Hadfield seems proud of its moment in the sun, the town's real-life local shops selling laminated illustrated maps that will point you in the direction of buildings used to represent Hilary Briss's butcher's shop and Pauline Campbell-Jones's job centre. The use of Hadfield as a filming location is cleverly and wittily foregrounded in the team's postmodern 2005 feature film spin-off *The League of Gentlemen's Apocalypse*, with the characters time slipping between Hadfield and its fictional counterpart via a door in the church crypt.

LOVE FEAST

In one of Derbyshire's remotest corners – Alport Castles, located off the Snake Pass road – every July on the first Sunday of the month a little-known and rarely documented ceremony is held in a stone barn – the Love Feast.

Anyone hoping from the name for some kind of 1960s communal free-love-style experience is likely to be sorely disappointed, for the Love Feast consists of a simple annual religious Methodist service held within the barn of Alport Castles Farm. Attendees sit on simple wooden benches, sing unaccompanied hymns and offer up testimonies. A two-handled 'loving cup' containing spring water is passed around for people to sip from alongside a communal fruit cake.

The Skelton family are the owners of Alport Castles Farm and therefore the current custodians of the tradition. Judy Skelton has amassed a wealth of material and reminiscences relating to the Love Feast online at woodlandschapel. wordpress.com.

An interesting historical footnote to the Love Feast is that Alport Castles Farm was the birthplace of Suffragette, social justice campaigner and magistrate Hannah Mitchell (née Wester) (1872–1956). One of six children, Mitchell did not get on with her mother, who was an ill-tempered woman who sometimes forced her children to sleep in the barn, and left home at age 14 after an argument to go and live with her brother in Glossop.

Mitchell's autobiography *The Hard Way Up* recalled the annual preparations for the Love Feast when she was a girl growing up on the farm:

> There were one or two red-letter days in the year which I love to recall. Chief among them was the annual Love-feast, an ancient religious festival held in high summer in my father's barn. This event was much thought of in the neighbourhood and indeed in many places much further afield. Weeks beforehand my mother spring-cleaned, papered and white-washed, we girls scrubbed and polished inside the house, while the boys painted the window frames and the house doors green. All the farm buildings were whitewashed inside, the doors painted a clean stone colour. The yard was swept, the gardens weeded, even the big stone water-trough was emptied and scrubbed, until when refilled it sparkled as if set with diamonds. On the day preceding the event, the big barn was emptied and swept, the floor strewn with rushes and bracken, rough planks supported by big stones arranged as seats; a trestle table served as a platform, the big Bible and hymn books from the Chapel were brought in, and all was ready. My mother baked bread, pies

Attendees of the Alport Castles Love Feast in 2019.

The 'loving cup' is passed around at the 2019 Love Feast.

and cakes, roasted a great piece of beef, and boiled a ham, while we got out the best china and table-linen and set tables in the parlour, or 'house-place', and in the big kitchen. On Sunday morning we rose early, for by nine o'clock the worshippers began to arrive, mostly on foot, as the big coaches from the distant towns had to be left at the end of the narrow lane. Groups of twenty or thirty arriving in this isolated spot seemed a multitude to us, who rarely saw a stranger from one year's end to another. Most of the visitors had left home so early they needed breakfast on their arrival, so all morning we were busy serving great pots of tea and jugs of milk and preparing the cold lunch, which was offered to all our friends and relatives.[52]

M

MATLEY, DOROTHY OF ASHOVER

Dorothy Matley was a seventeenth-century resident of the north-east Derbyshire village of Ashover employed in the local lead mining industry. Matley worked up on the surface at the top of a steep hill a quarter of a mile out of the village, armed with her tools of tub, sieve and hammer, and earned her living by breaking up chunks of ore brought from underground to separate out the lead content, as well as other minerals like fluorspar and calcite.

All accounts of Dorothy suggest a somewhat roguish character: she was known to use coarse language and have kleptomaniac tendencies. Her recurring protestation whenever caught in the act of pilfering was to utter words to the effect of, 'I would I might sink into the earth if it be so!' or, 'I would god make the earth open and swallow me up.'

One fateful day in March 1660 (or 1661 according to some sources), a young male colleague of Dorothy's removed his trousers so that they wouldn't get wet while he was at work and laid them to one side on the surface while working in his 'drawers'. Upon returning to his garments, he found the two pennies that had been in the pockets missing and accused the nearby Dorothy of having stolen them.

Enter to the scene at this point local man George Hodgkinson, 'a man of good report'[53] who just so happened to be passing the site of the disagreement. Other bit players on the scene are a small child stood by Dorothy's tub side, and another nearby child calling the first one to come away.

In response to the trouserless miner's allegations, Dorothy pulled her usual expression of faux-innocent indignation and trotted out one of her regular catchphrases.

Hodgkinson at this point in the proceedings was busying himself with ushering the child stood by Dorothy away from the scene and conveying her to her companion. For the next sequence of events I will here hand over to my melodramatic Victorian local newspaper journalist predecessor, relaying the story to the readers of the *Nottinghamshire Guardian* in 1883:

But, behold! They had not got above ten yards from Dorothy, but they heard her crying for help, so looking back, he saw the woman and her tub and sieve, twisting round, and sinking into the ground. Then said the man, 'Pray to God to pardon thy sin, for thou art never like to be seen alive any longer.' So she and her tub twirled round and round till they sunk about three yards into the earth, and there for a while staid. Then she called for help again, thinking, as she said, that she would stay there. Now [Hodgkinson], though greatly amazed, did begin to think which way to help her; but immediately a great stone, which appeared in the earth, fell upon her head and broke her skull, then the earth fell in upon her and covered her.[54]

Dorothy's body was subsequently recovered from the earth – with the young lead miner's stolen two pennies on her person.

Long before the *Fortean Times* and *Daily Star* appeared on the scene, the general public long had a thirst for tales of the unexplained, and the story of Dorothy's demise was accordingly written up and printed in a pamphlet published in London by W. Gilbertson in 1662, alongside a similarly remarkable incident from Yorkshire, under the snappy title *Two most strange wonders:*

The one is a true relation of an angel appearing to Mr James Wise minister in York-shire, and the many strange and wonderful visions which he at that time beheld; as also his prophecies concerning some years of plenty, and a great dearth presently afterwards to ensue; with the burning and utter destruction of many goodly towns and countries. The other being a most fearful judgment which befell Dorothy Matley of Ashover in the County of Derby on Saturday the 23. of March last, who having couzened a poor lad of two single pence, wish't that the ground might bury her alive if she had it, which presently came to pass, for the ground opened and swallowed her and the tub she washed lead-ore in. The truth of this wonder is here incerted by Mr. Iddolls minister; Tho. Riche, Henry Wapping kinsman to her, Giles Winter, Tho. Smith, Francis Brown and many others.

The incident sufficiently entered the popular consciousness of the time to the extent that it was picked up and recounted as a moral parable by *The Pilgrim's Progress* author John Bunyan in his book *The Life and Death of Mr Badman: An Analysis of a Wicked Man's Life, as a Warning For Others.*

The Ashover parish registers do indeed record the death of a Dorothy Matley, stating: '1660. Dorothy Matley, supposed wife of John Flint, of this parish foreswore herself; whereupon the ground open, and she sanke over March 1st; and being found dead she was buried March 2nd'[55] (note that here neither the date of the occurrence nor the year tallies with the pamphlet).

It will be down to the reader's own personal beliefs as to whether Dorothy's story is interpreted as unshakeable evidence of a form of divine judgement being meted out from on high – or just a case of a strange fluke and freak occurrence against the backdrop of unstable geological conditions caused by the many years of digging underneath Derbyshire for mining operations. In 1992 there was a similarly dramatic incident in a garden in Starkholmes above Matlock when an unfortunate combination of circumstances led to a huge crater opening up. The nearby Riber Mine had been operational until the 1950s and when the homeowner dumped some heavy quarry waste in their garden while doing some landscaping work they unknowingly crushed a clay culvert that the mineworkers had constructed underneath the ground.

A three-month period of biblical heavy rainfall a few years later subsequently led to an ever-growing hole in the newly landscaped garden, creating a self-developing water feature. This gradually filled up with water until it all quickly disappeared as the volume of water was forced underground. Fortunately the Big Hole of Starkholmes, as it came to be known, didn't swallow anyone up – but the water did sever an underground electricity cable, apocalyptically plunging all the residents of Starkholmes as well as Matlock Bath in the valley below into darkness.

MERMAIDS

Although Derbyshire is a landlocked county, mermaids have still managed to crop up at various sites over the years.

In the remote and awe-inspiringly bleak landscape around Kinder Scout, a mermaid is said to live in a pool close to the Kinder Downfall. According to local legend, she will appear at midnight on Easter Sunday and grant the gift of immortality to visitors upon whom she looks favourably; however, reader discretion is advised here, for if she takes a dislike to you then she may well drag you to your death in the depths of the Mermaids Pool. So an Easter visit to Kinder would be something of a lottery.

The *Derbyshire Courier* of 13 August 1842 reported how a local stir had been caused in Matlock Bath by the circulation of handbills promising the exhibition of a 'Wonderful Monster of the Deep'. As the paper reports:

The bill was accompanied with a verbal announcement that the monster, which was part fish, part man, and part mermaid, would be forthwith exhibited in the pool in the Old Bath [Hotel] yard. A crowd of persons speedily collected, and their attention while awaiting the arrival of the wonder of the deep was attracted to a gigantic fish basket, which was carried under the arm of one of the exhibitors, and from its bulk and apparent weight was supposed to contain the dinner or luncheon at least of the expected monster. The contents, however, proved to be of a different nature, as after some little delay, the aforesaid basket was opened, and was found to contain an object of no less importance than the wonder himself, who on making his appearance, was found to be no more or less than a young seal.

If the paper's account is to be believed, the locals appeared to take this deception with remarkably good humour:

Each one, of course, laughed at his neighbour being 'done', and the laughter thus becoming general, the proprietors of the exhibition were speedily forgiven for having assumed a travelling name and description for their marine rarity; and on his taking water, if the spectators were not absolutely astonished, it was quite evident that the roach and gudgeons were perfectly so. The animal was certainly a curiosity thus far inland, and his nimble evolutions in his accustomed element, and active though futile endeavours to make acquaintance with its finny inhabitants, excited considerable amusement. After dining on a little salmon and a few lamb chops *au naturel*, his amphibious monstership departed to astonish the inhabitants of the neighbouring towns.

It is hard to envisage a modern audience being quite as forgiving at having been swizzed in such a fashion and we can only imagine the scathing TripAdvisor reviews that might ensue.

For a guaranteed sighting of a fake mermaid, you can head to Buxton Museum and Art Gallery, whose 'Wonders of The Peak' exhibition has a specimen on display. It originally belonged to Dr William Medlycott Graham, who held the post of Chief Medical Officer of the Sierra Leone Government Railway in the late 1800s before moving on to become Director of Medical Research in Lagos by 1908. It is thought the doctor bought the 'mermaid' as a souvenir during his exotic travels, and it came to reside at Buxton via the Wellcome Institute for the History of Medicine, which was her home until 1982.

Research carried out on the Buxton mermaid by conservation staff at the University of Lincoln in 2012 revealed that it contains elements of a real fish tail, papier-mâché and human hair with teeth of carved bone and eyes of mollusc shell, so this mermaid, while a spurious fake, can still in all honesty be said to be part-fish, part-human.

MOB JUSTICE

If I had to sum up the village of Baslow in a single word, then the one I would probably plump for is 'genteel'. With its old-fashioned sweet shop, thatched cottages, cricket pitch, public footpaths leading on to the neighbouring Chatsworth estate and an average property selling price at the time of writing of £489,463,[56] Baslow is about as chocolate-boxy a village as you are likely to encounter in the north of England. One thing you certainly don't picture the Baslow of today as is a hotbed of scandal. Yet the *Derbyshire Times* of 17 December 1898 found itself reporting on 'lively doings' in Baslow: 'on Tuesday and Wednesday evenings, the town was in uproar'. The newspaper reporter had dutifully gathered all the gossip that led to this uproar:

It appears that a labouring man recently discarded his wife and adopted child, and went away with a young girl resident in the neighbourhood. This week the pair returned, and neighbours resolved to show their disapproval by giving a reception in which tin cans and other articles for making a discordant sound played a prominent part. On the Tuesday night, it is stated that several persons in the large crowd assembled outside the house, tried to force an entrance, the result being that the windows were broken and the door damaged. The couple were serenaded, the beating of tin cans and other noisy instruments continuing for some time. The following night two effigies were prepared and taken round the town in a wheelbarrow in front of a large number of people carrying torches. After the parade, the effigies were burned amidst the greatest excitement, the crowd numbering upwards of 200 people. There was a staff of police on duty, including P.C. Stevens, of Baslow, a sergeant from Stoney Middleton, and the Eyam constable, but they were not called upon to interfere, as the ringleaders and their supporters were careful not to infringe the law. It is some time since there was such a lively scene at Baslow, and the circumstances which caused it have been the sole topic of conversation amongst the inhabitants for the last few days.

The following week's edition of 24 December 1898 reported a further update with relish: 'I hear that the uproar was continued on Thursday night with even greater vigour. There was great beating of tin pots and cans, and, finally, an effigy was hung on a tree.'

Cyber bullying is a very real and distressing twenty-first-century concern but as this newspaper account shows us, if you were to transgress societal codes to the extent that you fell foul of popular opinion around the turn of the nineteenth and twentieth centuries then you could expect to be subject to a very public shaming from your local village community in a violent and sinister fashion, long before the internet was dreamed of. These public humiliations were usually referred to as a 'skimmington' or 'Ran Tanning'.

In his account of growing up in the village of Codnor in the Erewash Valley, Joseph M. Severn suggests that this form of community justice was more effectual than the police force of the time:

> There was a more effective way of keeping law and order amongst the villagers even than police supervision and court proceedings, which the village folk took into their own hands. But this pertained more especially, in cases of wife-beating, cruelty to children, persistent falling out with neighbours, and wife and family desertion. When it became known that a man had been beating his wife, thrashing or neglecting his children, or otherwise making his home life a nuisance; in fact, in any way wilfully disturbing the village security, or disturbing the peace, and his behaviour had become intolerable, arrangements were made for what is called in village parlance – Ran Tanning him. At an appropriate time, usually towards evening, when work was over, the organisers gathered together. Bill so-and-so was to be Ran Tanned! Every sort of discarded tray, bits of sheet iron, frying pans and tin cans of every description with good stout sticks and pokers, were brought into requisition: anything that would add to a general uproar and noise; when the culprits whereabouts were ascertained, a formidable procession was formed, and a manoeuvre made to get him well into the middle of the road; there was little chance then of his escaping, and the tumultuous shouting and march began. The noise and din was made unbearable. Whether he walked or ran he was kept in the middle of it, and marched through every street and road in the village. If by any chance he broke away, or bolted into a yard or entry, he was immediately hounded out and started afresh on the road. The procession gathered in size all along the way; men, women and children joined in by the score, sometimes hundreds, and after this unique punishment, which brought

him under the disapproving observation of all the village, he was set free, to return to his home, a wiser man, with less inclination to so offend again.[57]

Indeed, the local police were by no means immune from being on the receiving end of this treatment themselves, as the *High Peak News* of 6 October 1883 makes clear under the heading 'Taddington – Lynch Law':

> On Monday the 24th ult., this usually quiet village was roused, so it is stated, by reports that Police-constable Joe Harrison had amused himself by cruelly beating his wife, who is held in great respect in the village. This, so rumour hath it, not being his first offence in this respect, popular imagination ran riot, and on Tuesday afternoon he received a good 'ran-tanning' from young and not a few elderly men and women in the village. After this amusement had proceeded some time, an effigy of the 'bobby' was burnt in front of his own door. The play was kept up until a late hour in the evening. We hear that Police-constable Harrison contemplates removing to other and quieter quarters.

Barbara Haywood (née Pearce), born in Middleton-by-Wirksworth in 1919, chronicles the practice there in her memoir of village life, *A Rake Through the Past*. At Middleton, the punishment was more likely to be aimed at women of the village, and was augmented by the introduction of fire:

> 'Ran Tannin' – a mental chastisement – was an old village custom at Middleton in the last century. When a young girl, or woman had fallen from grace (that was how they would describe an illegitimate pregnancy), the men and youths laid a trail of straw along the High Street, poured paraffin on the straw and set it alight. As the trail of fire burned, these chauvinists marched up and down the street shouting and making an unearthly row, banging old tins and pan lids as they went.[58]

As Heywood quite rightly points out, it takes two to tango: 'The fact that one of their own sex had been involved was not a consideration, but of course, in those days, equality of the sexes was a long way in the future – and the "male" was lord and master.'[59]

The perceived offence that led to such a public spectacle erupting could sometimes seem a relatively trivial one. The *Derbyshire Courier* of 8 September 1885 reported on a public humiliation at Tideswell: 'At Bakewell Town Hall, on Friday, several men were charged with lighting a bonfire in the Market Place, at

Tideswell, and resisting and assaulting the village constable. About 300 persons assembled with the intention of burning the effigy of a tradesman named Howe,'[60] with musical accompaniment to the pyrotechnics provided by the Tideswell Band, who were also present. But what had Howe done to deserve such retribution? According to the report, he 'had incurred odium refusing the use of a large hall for the holding of the village flower show'.[61] Obviously the annual flower show was very important to Tideswellians! The paper chronicled how the police attempted to stamp out proceedings: 'The constable, Deakins, succeeded in carrying off the effigy while burning, and threw it into a cistern. The people took it out and again set it on fire, while the constable was held down and assaulted. It is alleged that the officer was struck across the face with tarred, burning faggots, and temporarily blinded. Edward Harrison Hill, who was charged with this offence, was remanded. For the minor offences the parties were fined nominal penalties.'[62]

Four years later they were at it again in Tideswell, the 7 October 1889 issue of the *Sheffield Independent* reporting:

On Saturday evening Tideswell was the scene of great excitement, it having been rumoured that two effigies – one of an old man 66 years and the other of a young girl 16 years of age – were to be burnt. The effigies were placed in a hand cart, and pulled through the streets followed by a crowd of people. When the residence of the girl's parents was reached the effigies were set ablaze. On account of the man's wife being ill the crowd kept away from the house as much as possible.[63]

The report does not really make the perceived misdemeanour clear but reading between the lines it would appear that the couple with a fifty-year age gap between them had entered into a relationship.

The production of the straw effigies of the perceived wrongdoers was often a recurring motif in the custom. S. O. Addy records that:

In 1888 a man and a woman living at Cold-Aston [Coal Aston], in Derbyshire, were engaged to be married. The wedding-ring was bought one Saturday, and the marriage was to be celebrated on the following Monday. But, in the meantime, they quarrelled, and the marriage did not take place. On the Monday evening the boys in the village made a straw image of the man, which they burnt in the street opposite to his door, and they also burnt a straw image of the woman opposite to her door in the same manner.[64]

Interestingly in this incident of a marriage falling through at the last minute, both the man and the women appear to have been viewed as equally culpable for the breakdown of the relationship. Addy adds in a footnote, 'This custom arose from the belief that the burning of the image would cause pain or death to the person whom it was intended to represent,'[65] in a similar fashion to a voodoo doll.

Addy explains the codes and conventions as practised at Coal Aston further:

> Lately, at the same place, when a man was 'ran-tanned', that is, when a straw image of him was made, and he rode in effigy, the image was taken round the village on three successive nights, and it was burnt on the last night. The carrying round of the image was accompanied by a number of people beating tin cans, and making a great din. It is said that if you carry the image round the village on three successive nights the man cannot 'have the law' of you. In this case the man had quarrelled with his wife, and the wife's friends caused the image to be made and carried round.[66]

This form of noisy public shaming persisted into the twentieth century. Under the headline 'Kirk Ireton: Remarkable Scenes', the *Ashbourne Telegraph* of 9 September 1904 reported:

> At the Wirksworth Petty Sessions on Tuesday, considerable time was occupied by hearing a number of summonses from Kirk Ireton for violent conduct so as to occasion a breach of the peace. The defendants were George Ford, Harry Gresley, Jas. Whittaker, sen., George Wood, and Geo. Smedley. Mr. Ducker (Derby), defended. It appeared from the evidence that the defendants, with some scores of others, proceeded to Blackwall House, the residence of a Mr. Tempest, who had by some means incurred their displeasure. They made a great noise with tin cans, buckets, &c. and carried an effigy, which they burnt in a field opposite Mr. Tempest's house. The bench considered the defendants were the ringleaders, and bound them over to keep the peace for three months in the sum of £5, and also to pay 7s. costs each.[67]

NAKED BOY RACING

Perhaps the unlikeliest of Derbyshire's traditions, which has now fallen into abeyance, is the traditional Naked Boy Racing that formerly took place in north Derbyshire. The best account of this bizarre sport is to be found in the January 1966 volume of *Derbyshire Life & Countryside* under the arresting headline 'The Naked Boys of Derbyshire' (I double-checked to make sure it wasn't the April issue to ensure that readers of the 1960s weren't being April Fooled).

The author of the article, Mary Forrest-Lowe, draws on writings left by an ancestor, Mr Forrest. While riding from Chesterfield to Worksop in the winter of 1755, Forrest chanced across huge crowds forming at Staveley. Upon making enquiries he was informed that 'the Naked Boys' were about to race a distance of 3 miles over the ice-covered ground.

Deciding this was something he simply must witness, Mr Forrest abandoned his journey and stayed to watch the racing, which was conducted from Staveley to Brimington and back by four naked youths, all aged around 16 and about 6ft tall. Upon establishing that a similar race was to be run the next day at Whitwell, Forrest – clearly by now a huge fan of Naked Boy Racing – checked into a local inn so he could see this remarkable spectacle a second time.

The following day crowds arrived from Sheffield, Derby, Mansfield, Chesterfield and Worksop to watch the race, which for the second day saw Whitwell native Flaxey Rotherham, 'the village idol', romp home to naked glory. His fellow racers appeared to have been good sports as they then hoisted Flaxey up on their shoulders and took him around the village in a naked victory parade that lasted an hour – all participants remaining nude throughout despite the freezing temperatures.

Mr Forrest's writings are backed up by Philip Kinder, who in his uncompleted history of Derbyshire written around the mid-seventeenth century, states:

> Their [i.e., Derbyshire folk] exercises, for the greate part, is the *Gymnopaidia*, or naked boy, an ould recreation among the Greeks, with this in foote-races,

you shall have in a winters day, the earth crusted over with ice, two agonists, stark naked, runn a foot race for 2 or 3 miles, with many hundred spectators, and the betts very small.

It was the joyless High Sheriff of Derbyshire who finally put a stop to this fine Derbyshire tradition in 1756 – the year after Mr Forrest's eyewitness account. If you still want to witness naked racing, you could visit Roskilde Festival in Denmark, which has an annual nøgenløb (naked race), or Australia's Meredith Music Festival where the 'Meredith Gift' nude race is staged – both are open to both male and female racers. Maybe the organisers of Derbyshire's Y Not? music festival held annually at Pikehall might consider introducing a similar element in future and in doing so revive a great lost Derbyshire sport?

Perhaps Tsvetelin Istatkov, originally hailing from Bulgaria but as of November 2019 living in Burton upon Trent (close to the border of Derbyshire and Staffordshire but just falling in the latter county) was attempting to revive this fine old local tradition on 2 November that year, when he caught a bus over the border into Derbyshire to visit Sudbury near Ashbourne.

Istatkov was subsequently spotted jogging through the grounds of the National Trust-owned property Sudbury Hall (home of the Museum of Childhood), '100 per cent completely naked, his genitalia were completely exposed',[68] according to a witness.

Istatkov was summonsed to appear before South Derbyshire Magistrate's Court, who heard an account of his bizarre behaviour in and around the grounds of the hall. The 23-year-old B&Q employee explained that a lot of 'bad things' had happened to him on the eventful day. Having got off the bus at Sudbury, he entered a park and was bitten on the hand by a dog. Andy Conboy, prosecuting, explained to the court, 'He took his top off trying to get rid of the dog. The dog then bit him on the leg and he takes his trousers off so the dog would let go.'[69]

Staff at Sudbury Hall were first made aware of Istatkov's presence when he was seen in the courtyard of the historic property minus his clothes and shouting. He was described in a newspaper court report as then 'jogging from west to east, heading in the direction of Sudbury village, before going over a garden fence [...] someone at the address came out, offering him a towel to put around him – but he came away from the house and back into the street.'[70]

He subsequently returned to the gardens of Sudbury Hall, where a staff member observed the defendant 'with his genitalia exposed shouting [a] one single-syllable sound'. Upon being asked to leave the grounds, Istatkov punched and headbutted the unfortunate member of staff, all while still naked.

For his eccentric actions Istatkov was given a two-year suspended sentence of twenty-four weeks in prison by magistrates, placed on the sex offender register for seven years, and ordered to pay costs of £85 and a £122 victim surcharge.

All a very far cry from the hero worship doled out to his naked running predecessor Flaxey Rotherham back in 1755.

OBSERVATORIES

A Derbyshireman, John Flamsteed (1646–1719), holds the distinction of being the first person to hold the title of Astronomer Royal in the United Kingdom.

Flamsteed recounts in his memoirs that he was 'borne [*sic*] at Denby, 5 miles from Derby, August 19, 1646 – my father having removed his family thither because the Sickness was then in Derby'.[71] This is a reminder that, whilst Eyam is the plague capital of Derbyshire, firmly lodged in popular consciousness as the site where the residents entered a voluntary quarantine during the years 1665–66 to stop the bubonic plague from spreading beyond the confines of the village, many other locations across the county were subject to similar outbreaks over the years.

In addition to the large-scale outbreak in the year of his birth referenced by Flamsteed, there are records of separate epidemics of plague in Derby in 1586, 1592–33, 1605 and 1665 (the same year that Eyam was first stricken). Chetwynd Leech (*Our County Town*, 1901), having compared the numbers of fatalities per head of population, highlights the fact that the 1665 Derby epidemic was proportionally equally as severe as the famous outbreak that ravaged London in the same year (the disease made its way up to Eyam from the capital via a package of cloth harbouring fleas carrying the disease that was sent up from London to the local tailor, George Viccars – consequently the first victim to die of the disease in the village). Leech also speculates that the macabrely named Deadman's Lane close to Derby train station was the site of a mass plague burial pit where the unfortunate victims were deposited.

Between October 1586 and November 1587, one in five people in Chesterfield died of the plague (recorded in the parish register as 'The Great Plague of Chesterfield'), with further outbreaks in the town in 1603 and 1608–09. At Belper in 1603, fifty-three residents died of plague, and at Ashbourne two years later sixty-two people succumbed. Brimington was the site of an outbreak in 1603 and Staveley in 1635. The parish register at Darley Dale recorded in July 1551 that nine locals had died as a result of 'ye sweatinge sicknesse'.

The plague situation in Derby had clearly abated by the time Flamsteed reached schooling age, as he was sent to the Derby School, an educational establishment that had a lengthy existence between the years 1160 and 1989. With the recommendation of the Master of Derby School, Flamsteed subsequently went on to study at Jesus College, Cambridge.

After Cambridge, Flamsteed was ordained as a deacon and was preparing to return to Derbyshire, but was waylaid to London by his patron, Jonas Moore, Surveyor-General of the Ordnance. In London he was introduced to King Charles II and subsequently inducted as an official Assistant to the Royal Commission. While astronomy had been practised in some form since ancient times, when Flamsteed arrived in London the Scientific Revolution of the sixteenth and seventeenth centuries was still in full sway.

Flamsteed died in 1719 and was interred at St Bartholomew's Church in Burstow, Surrey. His home county have honoured him in a number of ways, including the Derby and District Astronomical Society naming their observatory – which was constructed on farmland at Brailsford and opened in 1992 – the Flamsteed Observatory, and the John Flamsteed Community School in his home village of Denby also taking on his name (it was originally founded in 1894 as Smithy Houses School). A little further away from home, he also has a crater on the moon named after him.

A lesser-known name in the field of astronomy, but one who nonetheless also gave Derbyshire a remarkable legacy, is Chesterfield's Horace Barnett.

At the end of Hastings Close, an ordinary-looking cul-de-sac in the Chesterfield suburb of Newbold, can be found an unexpected facility: the Barnett Observatory, headquarters of the Chesterfield Astronomical Society. It was constructed on a former farmland site in the late 1950s and took three years to build, opening its doors in 1960.

The observatory was chiefly the vision of Barnett and he was the driving force behind the fundraising and building work, consequently it bears his name. During the period of building work the participants gained the affectionate nickname 'The Newbold Nutters' from local people in view of their zeal to complete the project of constructing an observatory themselves, seemingly against all the odds. The Society stages regular open evenings where members of the public are invited to squint through its 18in-diameter telescope (according to *The Sky at Night* magazine, the ninth largest amateur telescope in the UK) at the stars above.

Other Derbyshire observatories include one opened in 2017 at Queen Elizabeth's Grammar School, Ashbourne, and the Malcom Parry Observatory at Long Eaton School.

Horace Barnett inspecting the telescope at the Barnett Observatory, Newbold, Chesterfield, in 1960. Image reproduced by kind permission of Chesterfield Astronomical Society.

The Barnett Observatory at Newbold open to the public on one of their Friday evening sessions.

PADLEY MARTYRS

The story of the Padley Martyrs takes us back to the febrile atmosphere of the late sixteenth century. Against the backdrop of a feared Spanish Catholic invasion of England, to be ordained a Catholic priest abroad was at this time deemed a treasonous offence.

Padley Manor near Grindleford had formerly belonged to the Eyre family, but through the marriage of Anne Eyre to Sir Thomas Fitzherbert in 1534 it became Fitzherbert property — by 1588 it was occupied by Sir Thomas's younger brother, John. The Fitzherberts were a devout Catholic family who refused to attend Church of England services. It was this knowledge that in 1588 led to the hall being raided, and two itinerant Catholic priests were encountered hiding within the walls. The priests in question were Nicholas Garlick (born around 1555 at Dinting near Glossop and formerly a schoolmaster at Tideswell) and Robert Ludlum (born *c.*1551 at either Whirlow, Sheffield, or Radbourne near Derby).

The two priests were hauled away for trial at Derby on 23 July 1588, where they were found guilty of treason, receiving the consequent sentence of being hung, drawn and quartered, which was carried out the following day on St Mary's Bridge, Derby. Their heads and quarters were taken and displayed on poles around the streets of Derby, as was the custom of the time.

For his part in the matter John Fitzherbert was imprisoned and died in 1590. His brother Sir Thomas had been incarcerated for thirty-two years for his religious beliefs and died in the Tower of London the following year. The manor at Padley was seized by the Crown. It was subsequently returned to the Fitzherbert family, but because of the debts they had accrued subsequently had to be sold and from the mid century onwards began to fall into a ruinous state, leaving mainly only the building's foundations to last into the modern era.

The building that is now Padley Chapel was formerly the gatehouse to the hall, which survived intact into the twentieth century and had been used as a barn in which to keep cattle. In 1931 it was purchased by Charles Payne of

Above: The Padley Pilgrimage procession in the 1930s, from a glass lantern slide.

Left: The Padley Pilgrimage service in 2015.

the Diocese of Nottingham and converted into a chapel, with stained-glass windows depicting the martyrs installed.

Since 1898 an annual pilgrimage has been held in July that remembers the priests and their fates. Participants meet at Grindleford Railway Station before processing the short distance along woodland paths to the location of Padley Hall, then parking themselves among the foundation stones of the ruined building and listening to an open-air sermon. Garlick and Ludlum were among the eighty-five martyrs of England and Wales who were selected for beatification by Pope John Paul II on 22 November 1987.

POOR OLD HORSE

As we have previously seen with the Derby Tup (QV), in Derbyshire in days of yore nothing quite said 'It's Christmastime' like ganging together with a group of your mates, constructing a prop representation of a dead animal and going out and about giving a little performance as a way of raising funds to tide you over the holiday period.

Folklorist S.O. Addy (1907) remembers both the Old Tup and the Old Horse being performed in Dronfield and Norton (now part of Sheffield) when he was a boy 'about 1855'. There is a recording of the horse appearing in Staveley at a similar time, around 1865. Folk dance and drama collector William J. Shipley spoke to an unnamed old lady in 1931 who remembered a visit from the horse there when she was a young girl – an experience that frightened her. She recalls:

> They came into my farther's [sic] yard (he wouldn't allow them in the house for they were so rough) about Christmas time and first of all they set up a big horse, a wooden one – I believe it had wooden pegs for teeth – but I was so terrified at their grotesque caps and faces that I am not sure whether they carried it or not.[72]

The 'rough' participants in this escapade were referred to as 'Morris dancers'. Addy also remembers the horse as having a wooden head, although in other accounts a real horse's skull, sometimes painted up and with additions of a cloth tongue and bottle-top eyes, was employed.

In 1981, folklore researcher (and founding member of the revived Winster Guisers) Dave Bathe interviewed Jim Heath, then aged 74, who lived with his parents in New Whittington until around 1919, when at the age of 12 he moved to Holymoorside, where his father took over Yew Tree Farm. Bathe's interview notes record how at Christmas time the local butcher's shop at New Whittington run by his father (J. W. Heath) supplied 'local lads and men (anything from 20 to 56 – and younger?) with cows' and sheep's skulls and cleaned-up horses skulls for use in a Christmas "visiting" custom'. Heath described the arrival of the 'Horse':

> You used to hear a knock at the door, and the trick then was to heat up some pennies in the oven and when you gave them to them they used to jump about saying 'ow!' Well, these lads used to be singing and you'd open the door and there was this thing (horse's head) snapping at you![73]

Another source of horses' heads was Clayton's Knacker's Yard, a tannery in Chesterfield:

> It was a regular thing – he used to expect them at Christmas time. The horses used to be specially slaughtered so as to leave the head undamaged (the means of slaughter was a sledge hammer) and the head cut off cleanly. The flesh would then be burnt off, leaving some hide on the head. Then they used to go to John Green's timber yard at Whittington Hill and 'he used to fix the heads up for them'. When the head was taken round 'sometimes the eyes were lit up – with a carriage candle cut in two, and put in the eye holes – sometimes we used to do that for them.' The cows' (and sheeps') heads were prepared for the 'gangs' (Jim's term) by Jim and his father. The boys in the shop usually had the job of dealing with animal heads, i.e. skinning, cutting off cow's cheeks, tongue, brains, etc. For the gangs at Christmas the cows (or sheep) would be killed without damaging the head, which after cleaning would be boiled up in the boiler until the bones were clean. The skulls were collected by the 'lads' or men when dry and then painted and decorated to suit [and fixed onto] a 'mast' construction [with] a 'cloth' or cover being fixed to the head and covering the back of the performer, who would crouch down behind the head.[74]

Heath told Bathe that 'several "gangs"' used to go around with horses or cows heads at Christmas, including New Whittington, Handley and other places, and related 'an anecdote about how Tom Freeman (the carter) chased one "horses' head" gang with a double-barrelled shotgun (in jest?) – they ran, and left the head behind'.[75]

A lively record of the Horse being performed at Coal Aston comes from the reminiscences of coal miner Joseph Sharpe, as written down by Nellie Connole in the years 1932–36 and published as *Dark at Seven – The Life of a Derbyshire Miner* in 1988. Sharpe was one of the team who went out performing the Horse, and describes the preparations involved in the making of their essential prop:

> If we knew where a horse had died or been buried we used to go and fetch the head, then we used to boil it until the flesh dropped off its bones. When it was dry it was ready for wiring and we wired it so that the jaws would move and its mouth open. That done, we painted round its lips and nostrils red and fixed in its mouth a tongue of red flannel. Next we put in the painted glass eyes, mounted the head on a stick with a little stick across to manipulate it, found a cloth and we were all fixed.[76]

As recalled by Sharpe, the performance, which took place in the midwinter gloom, was a strange, almost supernatural ritual, which could have unpredictable effects on those that witnessed it:

> We began with a mimicry of horse and rider, going through all the motions and making it as realistic as possible. It was a strange, weird dance and has a wonderful effect as vivid and lifelike as it was ghostly. Oh! You needed good nerves to enjoy it.[77]

The previous generation, Sharpe's father induced similarly dramatic results on a visit to Barlow when they took the horse up to the pit cabins one night to frighten 'Old Jack', a local who reckoned himself unfrightenable:

> When they reached Waterloo cabin they made certain he was in, then they poked the horse's head round the piece of sacking that served as a door. Someone moved the stick and the scarlet jaws gaped open revealing the bare white bones inside and the lolling blood red tongue. The Old Horse moved this way and that; its mouth opening and closing; the painted eyes gleaming in its black, glistening skeleton of a face. Old Jack, who boasted that nothing could frighten him, was crouched near the fire staring in abject terror at the apparition. He shouted crazily at the thing and while he stared and shouted he was groping behind his back for the poker. Then giving way utterly to his fright he tried to clamber up the chimney. The practical jokers then thought

they had gone far enough and, going in, they tried to quiet him but they could not. They told him what it was but still he shouted and screamed at them. Nothing could stop him and now, thoroughly alarmed, the men sent for a doctor. When the doctor came he said old Jack would be alright but some of them must stay and watch him for at least a day. So my father and one or two of his pals spent a not very merry Christmas looking after a man they had very nearly driven insane.[78]

A more tragic incident than this concerning a Poor Old Horse performance occurred during the Christmas period of 1868–69. The *Derbyshire Times* of 20 February 1869 reported on the discovery of a body in the River Derwent at Baslow Bridge the previous Saturday. The body belonged to James Greenwood, a 31-year-old collier from Dronfield, and was removed to the Green Man Inn, where an inquest was held. The jury heard that the body had been in the water for some time. Greenwood was identified by his brother, John, who had last seen James on the Wednesday after Christmas Day at Dronfield, where, as the paper reported, 'he was coming as a "guiser", or with what is termed in country places as the "old horse" or "ball"'.

The guising troupe, which consisted of six others as well as Greenwood, had performed the Old Horse at the Bull's Head Inn, Calver, on New Year's Day 1869. The landlord of the Inn, Isaac Bradwell, reported that the party arrived at around eight o' clock and performed 'Ball'; at that point 'they were not very sober'. Having been provided with refreshments by Bradwell in exchange for their performance, they stayed at the inn and continued to drink at their own expense. Fuelled by booze, internal tensions began to emerge within the team, and eventually they became quarrelsome. William Broomhead, present at the pub on the night in question, gave evidence that 'between ten and eleven o' clock at night, [the] deceased was wrangling with one of the party, who would not take much notice, and challenged him out to fight. [...] When they got out of the door they both put themselves in a fighting attitude and two blows were struck by each party. Then the deceased went up to his opponent and asked what cause they had to fight? And no reply was given, and that ended the fight.' Following this fracas, which fizzled out to nothing, Greenwood told Broomhead he was going home and took himself off in the direction of Calver Bridge. On top of being worse the wear for drink, James was near-sighted, and it was the coroner's belief that he had fallen over an embankment into the river at Calver Bridge and would have been unable to scramble to safety by himself. The verdict: 'Found drowned'.

The newspaper reported Greenwood as having a 'good character in his own neighbourhood, [and] has left a widow and two children to lament his untimely end'. It is worth taking a moment here to note that Greenwood's native Dronfield, where he had set off for home on foot late at night in order to perform this midwinter custom to earn himself and his pals a bit of money to tide them over the Christmas holidays, is over 10 miles away from Calver.

The Poor Old Horse was performed locally by a team from Dronfield until the early 1970s, when they were too elderly to continue and no one else was willing to take on the mantle. They used to perform at houses at Dore on the edge of Sheffield on New Year's Day, taking the horse prop with them on the bus!

Dave Bathe's calls to the local press in the early 1980s seeking information about guising and mumming in Derbyshire drew a response from a Mrs C Ralphs, a member of the family of one of the performers as witnessed by Greig in the previous decade:

> The Old Horse which you so rightly say was a decorated horses head set on a skull, is at the moment at my Mother & Father-in-law's house. Although now it has died out as many of the men who went round the pubs and houses have become elderly or died. My father-in-law was one of these men who acted out the 'Poor Old Horse'.[79]

It was a bit of a long shot given that it was now over thirty years down the line, but I contacted the Old Dronfield Society to see if they knew anything about the horse custom, and more to the point, the whereabouts of the horse used. I received a reply from Jean Kendall from the Society (recently amalgamated with the Dronfield Heritage Trust, and based at the fifteenth-century Hall Barn in the town). The Horse custom was viewed with great fondness by the group, and it transpired that in the early 1990s at their instigation the horse itself was retrieved from the loft of the Ralphs family home, where it was still in storage. In winter 1990–91, and again in 1992, the custom was revived with performances given for members of the Old Dronfield Society, which were recorded to video. But then following these two performances there followed something of a mystery. The horse vanished, leading to Jean putting out an appeal in an edition of the *Dronfield History Miscellany*: 'Unfortunately, the whereabouts of the Poor Old Horse are not known. We hope it has found a safe home somewhere. If anybody knows what became of it, please get in touch.'

Members of the Old Dronfield Society perform the Poor Old Horse in 1991 using the horse that had been in storage for two decades – after this photograph was taken, it mysteriously vanished! Image reproduced by kind permission of Dronfield Heritage Trust.

Poor Old Horse reimagined for the twenty-first century in a performance by students of Dronfield Henry Fanshawe school of a script by Eoin Bentick and Rob Thomson.

Although the disappearance of the original horse was a shame, the custom was still remembered with fondness in Dronfield and a chance sighting of a horse's skull in an antique shop led to the idea of some sort of revival. The First Arts organisation put out an open call with a budget of £4,500, which was awarded to scriptwriters Rob Thomson and Eoin Bentick. They worked with students from Dronfield's Henry Fanshawe school and interviewed elderly residents of local care homes to produce a short play of around fifteen minutes' duration with musical accompaniment, which was performed in the Peel Centre on 2 December 2016 as part of Dronfield's annual Christmas lights switch-on event. The horse itself made an appearance towards the end of the performance, entering from a side door and lumbering briefly around the room waving its broomstick arms, standing erect on two legs rather than being operated from underneath a cloak by a crouched performer. The overall effect was more akin to a Welsh Mari Lwyd (a New Year's custom found in South Wales also involving a performer with a horse's skull) than the Dronfield horse of old, and the whole thing could probably be more accurately described as a 're-interpretation' of the tradition rather than a 'revival'.

The play that was devised explored themes of isolation and social isolation, with the Horse custom as a background framework. This was performed by a troupe of half a dozen teenage girl drama students from the Henry Fanshawe school. Part of the plot concerned one of the girls being dared to steal the horse's head. Throughout, a teenage boy improvised a soundtrack with an electric guitar fed through numerous effects pedals.

The Christmas horse visits also took place at Ashford-in-the-Water, Eyam and Little Hucklow. As noted in the *Derbyshire Times* report into James Greenwood's death, in these villages the horse was given the name of 'Ball'. J.B. Firth in *Highways and Byways of Derbyshire* (1905) says this is one of several ancient Eyam customs that had only recently died out at his time of writing. He describes the house-visiting custom as 'a mysterious game called Ball, which consisted of dragging about from house to house the figure of a horse, lit up with candles placed in its inside. It was wheeled into the kitchens to the accompaniment of a song.'[80]

QUARNDON SPA

While Derbyshire has been a Mecca for tourists ever since the concept of people travelling around for reasons of leisure has existed, one notable deficiency it experiences as a landlocked county is its lack of a coastline. Perhaps to compensate for this, places like Buxton and Matlock developed as fashionable inland spa destinations. The vogue for 'taking the waters' petered out as the twentieth century progressed: it has been suggested that the foundation of the National Health Service in 1948 and the consequent provision of universal healthcare for all using the latest scientific knowledge available was the final nail in the coffin for people travelling up to Matlock at their own expense to subject themselves to the resort's fresh air and water treatments at the hydros, which were by this point in time beginning to struggle to attract custom and had come to be perceived as outdated relics of a bygone era. The collapse of interest in the hydros left Matlock littered with many large, grand Victorian buildings that formed the premises of the various hydropathic hotels, which have subsequently been repurposed for a variety of uses including accommodation, a teacher training college, care homes, and in the former Smedleys premises – the largest and grandest of all the hydros – the headquarters of Derbyshire County Council.

As well as these famed spa resorts, Derbyshire had several more obscure sites that people would visit in former days to imbibe or bathe in the local waters because of their perceived qualities. Bakewell derives its name from a spring or well associated with a woman named Badeca or Beadeca and was developed around the location of twelve thermal mineral water springs. A bath house was subsequently built there in 1697 by the Duke of Rutland (thus predating the Buxton expansion scheme of the 1780s overseen by his aristocratic neighbour at Chatsworth, the Duke of Devonshire), but it never really took off as a spa destination. The bath house is still there, forming the twentieth-century premises for the local branch of the Royal British Legion Club, and the bath remains in the building's vaulted basement. Its post-bathing uses have ranged from the pedestrian (a storage facility) to the slightly more bizarre (a small mushroom farm).

The south of the county also had sites that were marketed for their bathing potential. By 1768 the *Derby Telegraph* was highlighting the facilities of 'a new erected handsome Stone Building over the Wells, with commodious inclos'd Baths for the separate Accommodation of Gentlemen and Ladies' at Quarndon, a few miles from the town (as it still then was) centre of Derby.

The waters at Quarndon came from chalybeate springs – in other words, water that contained traces of iron salts. They were said, according to a writer of 1663, to be 'good against vomiting, comforts ye stomach, cures ye ulcers of ye bladder, stops all fluxes, helps conception and stays bleeding in ye breast'.[81] Celebrated visitors who imbibed the waters at Quarndon include dictionary compiler Samuel Johnson and, in 1727, Daniel Defoe, passing through Derbyshire as part of his travels around the country, which were written up and published as *A Tour Thro' the Whole Island of Great Britain*. Defoe praised the water itself at Quarndon, but grumbled about the poor standard of lodgings and lack of quality entertainment in the village.

Defoe's complaints offer a clue as to Quarndon spa's decline in fortunes: while many people walked the 3 miles from Derby to take its waters, it simply did not have the same level of facilities as Buxton or Matlock to keep the smart set sufficiently entertained. By the close of the nineteenth century the formerly handsome stone wellhouse had fallen into a state of disrepair and the spring had almost dried up.

RIVALRIES

Laurence Ramsbottom, Secretary of the Derbyshire Rural Community Council, writing in a book produced in 1934 as a souvenir of a conference held by the National Association of Headteachers at Buxton, issued a note of warning to attendees regarding the locals:

> It is a fact that Derbyshire villagers still take unkindly to those who come to settle among them, yet they display a warm-hearted kindness to all who come as visitors. They resent 'foreigners' who desire to live and work among them, and this resentment has been carried to strange excesses in many parts. 'Tarring and feathering' has been known even in quite recent years [...] Though my own welcome in all Derbyshire villages has been one of real kindness and cordiality, one can find many evidences still of the suspicion of the 'foreigner,' especially if he [sic] attempts to settle in the village.[82]

There could often be a sense of great and long-lasting enmity build up between neighbouring villages. The population of previous centuries was less mobile, with it being much more common for people to live out their lives and die in the village into which they were born. S.O. Addy, writing in 1895, relates that, 'I have heard people say that, fifty years ago and more, there was much rivalry in Derbyshire between one village and another. The inhabitants of one village, especially boys, would regard those living in an adjacent village as foreigners.'[83]

Addy had first-hand experience of this kind of opprobrium meted out to outsiders: 'If a boy went into another village he would be attacked by the boys living there, and I have been stoned myself when going through a village to which I did not belong.'[84] He highlights the neighbouring villages of Dore and Totley (both formerly Derbyshire villages that have since the 1930s become subsumed into suburbs of the South Yorkshire city of Sheffield as the city boundaries have expanded). Like opposing teams on either side of a football stadium, the local lads had a particular chant that was hurled at their rivals whenever they encountered each other:

There was great rivalry between the boys of Dore and Totley, who used to revile each other, the Dore boys saying:

Totley bugs,
Water-clogs,
Water-porridge and hardly that.

The Totley boys replied:

Dore bugs,
Water-clogs,
Eating out o' swill-tubs,
Up a ladder and down a wall,
A penny loaf will serve you all.[85]

The 'up a ladder and down a wall' line of the Totley boys' chant is a reference to an obscure local belief that for some reason the people of Dore objected to living in houses with chambers or staircases in them, and residents used to get to their bedrooms at night by shinning up iron pegs driven into the wall in preference to ascending stairs. Now a highly desirable neighbourhood and home to many a professional sportsperson, it is hard to envisage that anyone in Dore still does this. And if you're reading this and tutting at all the boisterous behaviour, it turns out the girls were even worse – Addy also informs us that there were a corresponding set of verses the girls of Dore and Totley used to fling at each other, but that they are 'too coarse to quote', although he hints they 'imputed gross unchastity to each other', so we can make a fairly reasonable guess at the gist.

Local folklore collector Angela Barton of Loundsley Green, Chesterfield, documented a similar sense of rivalry in days of yore between the locals of Barlow and Newbold in a 1975 letter to fellow folklorist Charlotte Norman (Newbold is nowadays a suburb of Chesterfield as the town has expanded outwards, but Barlow remains a distinct entity). Barton writes:

There used to be village feuds. In the days of my grandfather (around the turn of the [nineteenth/twentieth] century) there was such a feud between

Barlow and Newbold (about 6 miles apart). If Newbold men had to go through Barlow they went in a group, otherwise they would be set upon. […] The Barlow people referred to the Newbold-ites as 'Newbold-soft watter [water] town'. This referred to the fact that the Newbold people had rain butts to catch water, unlike Barlow which had its wells […] The rallying cry for the Newbold-ites entering Barlow was 'Newbold for ever' and this provocative cry was in the nature of a challenge to the residents to do their worst.[86]

Despite the fact that since the time Barton refers to a piped water supply into the majority of households has become commonplace, Barlow still takes a sense of pride in its wells, dressing them annually in August for their well dressing ceremony. Here, unlike the majority of Derbyshire well dressing sites who use individual flower petals, the technique is to use whole flower heads when producing the dressings, which are in triptych form.

Given this sense of local pride bordering on insularity, romances that developed between a local person and an 'outsider' could be a thorny issue, and there were formerly various complex social codes in place that nowadays would seem unthinkable. Addy records:

A Barlow well dressing *c.*1900 photographed with local men who were presumably involved with designing and executing it.

At Bradwell, and other villages in the Peak of Derbyshire, young men who courted girls residing outside the limits of their own township had to pay a fine, called 'cock-walk' or 'foot-ale', to the young men in whose township such girls resided. This fine was 1s. 6d. at Bradwell; in some places it was 1s. If the fine was paid, the interloper was permitted to go free and unmolested. But if the interloper refused to pay, a halter was put round his neck and he was driven round the village. The money was divided by the young men who exacted the fine, and it was usually spent in drink.[87]

The *High Peak Chronicle* of 2 December 1909 records another punishment that a young man from outside a village dating a local girl could have been subjected to: 'pitchering', which consisted of being thrown into a well.

There was a long-running dispute between the neighbouring White Peak villages of Winster and Elton, both of which, until the closure of the Mill Close Mine in the 1930s, formerly had a high volume of residents employed in the local lead mining industry. Such was the undercurrent of bubbling disdain

All Saints Church, Elton, showing the clock that was installed in 1870; miners from the neighbouring village of Winster 'helpfully' offered to assist their Eltonian counterparts get to grips with telling the time.

between the villages that even something as seemingly innocuous as the village church gaining a clock could spark off open contempt, as the *High Peak News* of 5 July 1883 reported in its 'Echoes from the Derbyshire Hills' column:

> subscriptions to the amount of £70 have been raised for the purpose of placing a clock in the tower of Elton Church. The clock is being made by Mr. Ellerby, of Ashbourne. Some rough chaff has recently been passed between the Winster and Elton miners as to their respective abilities. The former, with some degree of modesty, contend that they are the most intelligent of their crew for miles round; and in proof of this they have generously offered, when the new clock is raised, at Elton, to instruct the miners of that place in the art of time-telling.[88]

RODGERS, PHILIP OF GRINDLEFORD

Grindleford is a rather sleepy Peak District village lying less than 10 miles from the centre of Sheffield, and ever since the opening of the village's railway station in 1894 (happily, this particular railway line escaped the Beeching cutbacks of the 1960s and is still functional in the twenty-first century) it has proved a popular rural base for many who commute into the South Yorkshire city for work. It does not immediately exude the air of a place likely to produce a remarkable visionary with the apparent ability to communicate with beings from other worlds – and yet one local man claimed to have the power to do just that.

Philip Rodgers was born in 1916, into a musical family – his mother had sung in the early days of the radio, and his father was a Sheffield choirmaster; Philip himself went on to learn to play the recorder to a professional standard, being classed as one of the top three most proficient musicians of the instrument in Europe and, like his mother, consequently appearing as a performer on BBC radio and other European networks. He was born with a visual impairment, so as a child was sent to a Rudolph Steiner school, which like all establishments of that ilk focused on creative learning and play at an unhurried pace. In 1956 Rodgers read the book *Inside the Space Ships* by George Adamski, which had been published the year before and purportedly detailed first-hand accounts of extraterrestrial abduction. Shortly after reading the book a strong 'hunch' compelled Rodgers to climb Grindleford's Sir William Hill one evening, where he saw pulsating coloured lights in the night sky that he referred to as a 'cosmic ophthalmoscope'. He subsequently had several similar experiences on the hill but his friends were sceptical as to what he had seen in view of his limited vision.

From 1957 onwards the visual experiences that Philip attributed to extraterrestrial craft visiting the Peak District were joined by various auditory phenomena characterised as 'a loud metallic note changing in intensity but not pitch', 'singing discs' and an 'ecstatic chorus with the air full of noises'.[89]

Given that Philip was beginning to experience these otherworldly noises with a degree of intensity, on the evening of 24 November 1957 he decided to try to capture them on tape and so placed his Grundig tape recorder on his bedroom windowsill. Rodgers himself described the results as follows:

> After a few minutes I was rewarded with a peculiar, penetrating, whistling sound, seemingly coming from behind the ash tree on the other side of our lane. Immediately I ran indoors and rewound the tape, fully expecting there to be nothing on it. But, to my intense relief, there was the sound as clear as a bell. I noticed a peculiar, rising, double fundamental note, quite alien to any sound I had heard on Earth. That was my first recording of a sound believed to emanate from outer space …[90]

Philip continued his tape recording experiments over the winter of 1957–58, managing to capture in February 1958 what he viewed as breakthrough: 'several dulcimer-like bleeping sounds, in between which appeared the voice of a small girl shouting "Howdy"'.[91] This recording was swiftly followed on 21 March with one that captured 'a mechanically produced computer voice, saying faintly, "ship is real, people" against a background of clicking, resembling the noise of a typewriter'.[92] Philip interpreted this latest recording as being a 'terse' message that he took to mean 'that space ships are real and piloted by people'.[93]

Rodgers' deep musical knowledge meant that he was able to catalogue the sequences of noises his tape recorder picked up in a very specific and precise way, as seen in the way he describes this recording that was received shortly after the terse message in March:

> I picked up a fantastic series of musical sounds, mostly of instruments unknown to Earth. In particular they seemed very keen on demonstrating a method of tuning. One appeared to be a violin-like instrument, tuned in fifths, but with no G-string and, in its place an upper B (a fifth above the top E of a terrestrial violin). In between playing, they keep shouting greetings. There was also a strange harp-like instrument, improvising on strings, tuned to a somewhat 'modernistic' chord. Finally there came what sounded like a

goose, flying slowly through the air and emitting a peculiar booming sound as it approached. This, however, resolved into the voice of a woman with a rich mezzo-contralto quality and singing a type of slow chant, somewhat eerie, but nevertheless warm, human and utterly feminine.[94]

In among the recognisable language picked up on tape were more unusual pronouncements such as 'Yar-du-par-du', 'Nyanna-poddo', 'Ya-ba-huseta', 'Hiroshidu', 'Driota', and what Rodgers described as 'a very amorous sounding lady' saying, '"Mee-see-mah", followed by a self-conscious giggle'. Rodgers sent these examples and others to the BBC Languages Department at Caversham to have them analysed; the response came back that they resembled no known languages on Earth. BBC presenter Alan Whicker went to visit Rodgers at his Grindleford home accompanied by a *Tonight* camera crew to speak to him about his unusual recordings.

From the intense period of activity during the late 1950s when Rodgers first began capturing strange auditory phenomena that arrived thick and fast from the aether surrounding his Grindleford home, the messages eventually began to tail off in frequency. In 1962 he only managed to make one recording, and by the mid-1960s was only managing to capture anything very infrequently. In attempting to sum up his unique and surreal experience, Philip wrote:

> I think of the Space People as coming here to welcome us back to an immense interplanetary union. Having studied us for thousands of years, they know only too well that they have to break down enormous barriers of ignorance, hostility, superstition and scepticism. They try every means within their power to contact us, to make various people interested, and to give us some small idea of their knowledge and wisdom. They show themselves in the sky. They seek out privileged individuals, some of whom they take up in their space craft. To me they have transmitted hundreds of tape recordings to analyse and study. My conclusion is first of all that the Space People exist; and secondly that their intentions towards our planet are friendly.[95]

Unfortunately, none of Philip Rodgers' remarkable tape recordings survived after his death, apart from a small snippet known as the 'Children's Party' (as it contained among other noises a mixture of apparently happy child-like voices). A murky second-generation copy of this segment survives as Philip played it at a public talk he gave in 1970 that was itself recorded.

SALT, MICAH, BUXTON ANTIQUARY

The epically named Micah Salt was born over the border in the Staffordshire Peakland village of Alstonefield in 1847. By the time of the 1881 census he had moved to the nearby market town of Buxton and established himself in business as a tailor.

While it was his tailoring that paid the bills, Salt has earnt his entry in *The A–Z of Curious Derbyshire* through indulging his passion for archaeology. This was unusual for the period he operated in, as at the time this pursuit was still mainly one that was pursued by the leisured class – an information panel at Buxton Museum notes that Salt was referred to with a slight sense of scorn in a journal of the time as 'an intelligent tradesman'. Salt, however, found himself in a fortuitous location to carry out his hobby, as the Peak District was clearly an area of important activity in prehistoric times and the landscape surrounding Buxton consequently a kind of giant lucky dip of historic artefacts just waiting to be excavated.

Noteworthy sites in and around the town where Salt performed excavations were at the Bull Ring henge at Dove Holes; Thirst House Cave, Deep Dale, where numerous Roman artefacts were found; Five Wells chambered tomb on Taddington Moor; Grin Low hill, and Fairfield Low, where he found the burial remains of three humans (the Low is encircled by trees that are known locally as 'Skeleton Wood' or 'Skellybob Wood', and is said by locals to retain a mysterious atmosphere in the modern era).

Salt bequeathed many of his finds to Buxton Museum on his death in 1915 and several remain on permanent display to this day. Salt carried his enthusiasm with him beyond the grave in a somewhat quirky fashion: his gravestone in Buxton Cemetery, carved from Derbyshire gritstone, stands out from the surrounding headstones as it is a replica of the large Saxon incised Celtic cross found in Eyam churchyard.

Ancient Runic Cross. Eyam Churchyard.

Above: The gravestone of local amateur archaeologist Micah Salt in Buxton Cemetery, a replica of the Saxon-era one to be found in Eyam churchyard.

Left: Postcard by R. Sneath of Sheffield showing the original Celtic cross at Eyam upon which Salt modelled his memorial.

SHEEP

The sheep is strongly bound up in the cultural life and folk traditions of Derbyshire.

A ram can be found propping up the shield on the county's coat of arms along with a stag, or in the bizarrely poetic language of heraldry, 'On the dexter side a Stag and on the sinister side a Ram both proper each gorged with a Chain Or pendent therefrom a Rose Gules surmounted by another Argent both barbed and seeded proper.'

Derby County football club have employed a ram in their insignia from 1924 onwards, resulting in the team's nickname, The Rams. The ram is also the emblem of the Sherwood Foresters Regiment, who since 1923 have held an annual pilgrimage on the first Sunday in July to the Foresters Memorial at Crich Stand, accompanied by a real-life lamb mascot. Traditionally, since 1912 the Duke of Devonshire has supplied the regiment with their mascot, from the Chatsworth flock of Swaledales.

It is thought that sheep were first introduced to Derbyshire around 3000 BC, becoming a particularly prominent feature of the landscape from the twelfth century onwards, when they were intensively and lucratively farmed on lands belonging to monastic granges like One Ash Grange near Monyash and Mouldridge Grange at Pikehall until the dissolution of the monasteries by Henry VIII in the sixteenth century.

Tideswell's St John the Baptist Church was the unlikely scene for a dramatic incident in either 1250 or 1251, when a dispute between Lichfield Cathedral and Lenton Priory erupted into sheep-related violence. Tideswell parish had formerly been granted to Lenton Priory by the Peverel family, but after William Peverel the Younger was accused of treason, the lands belonging to the family in the Peak District were seized by the crown and donated by King Henry II to his son, John. When John later became King John (of Magna Carta fame), he allocated the lands to the Bishop of Lichfield. Lenton Priory didn't accept this decision, and several hundred years of dispute followed, including a number of trials heard at the Vatican Court. In the early 1250s the monks of Lenton took matters into their own hands. Behaving in rather un-monk-like fashion, they burst into the church at Tideswell, where the Bishop of Lichfield had ordered sheep, lambs and wool be stored for safekeeping. A bloody brawl ensued during which eighteen of the lambs were killed and more injured by the rampaging monks, or crushed under their horses' hooves; the raiders succeeded in carrying off fourteen more live lambs as bounty.

Sheep washing demonstration by local farmers in the River Wye at Sheepwash Bridge, Ashford-in-the-Water, as part of the 2017 well dressing festival.

A well-known Derbyshire landmark is Ashford-in-the-Water's Sheepwash Bridge, which incorporates a stone-walled pen to hold sheep. Here, as part of the village's annual summer well dressing festivities, a demonstration of traditional sheep washing in the River Wye is given. In an age before chemical sheep dips, the creatures would have been dunked in the fast-flowing river waters to remove grit, dirt and grease from their fleeces prior to being shorn, so that the sheared material was easier to work when subsequently being transformed into wool.

Wingerworth near Chesterfield still has its well-preserved sheepwash dating from the mid-nineteenth century, which was in use until at least the 1920s. It provides one of the sites for Wingerworth's annual well dressings in early August. At Middleton-by-Youlgrave the village's former sheepwash is also pressed into service during well dressing time: here the boards containing clay are submerged in the sheepwash to soak beforehand so that the flower petals pressed into the clay survive longer. Different well dressing locations have their own interpretations of which natural materials are deemed permissible for inclusion in their own designs, but it is not uncommon to see sheep's wool worked into the tableaux, often being employed for clouds.

In the days when livestock were driven across the country to market on foot, most villages would have had their own pinfold, a circular stone enclosure where stray animals were locked up and kept at the expense of the owner and released upon payment of a fine to the Pinder, who was employed by the local Lord of the Manor. Examples survive at Barlow, Birchover (now incorporated into a private garden), Curbar, Hope, Milltown near Ashover, and on the Osmaston estate.

Another procedure in the area for returning any stray sheep to their owners was the annual Shepherd's Meet at Saltersbrook near Dunford Bridge. The *Buxton Advertiser* of 3 August 1870 reported on 'The Shepherds Festival on the Moors':

> The annual festival of restoring the lost or strayed sheep which has been held for more than two hundred years took place at Saltersbrook on the borders of the Yorkshire, Cheshire and Derbyshire moors during the past week. Amongst the visitors who witnessed the ceremony was the Lord Bishop of Chester. There was a large attendance of keepers and shepherds who brought with them over one hundred sheep, all of which were restored.

'Come-bye': the 2016 Longshaw Sheepdog Trials. They have been held annually since 1898.

A 1908 postcard (reproduced in Alan Bower's *Work and Play — from a Collection of Old Postcards of Derbyshire*) of the 'Shepherd's Demonstration' held at Chapel-en-le-Frith shows a public square rammed with townsfolk dressed in their smartest attire. Here the practical matter of returning lost sheep to their owners provided a backdrop for festivities. These 'demonstrations' were held in July and November. Flags are hanging from buildings, banners are held aloft, and groups of children in the foreground are holding what appear to be miniature maypoles with hooped garlands covered with flowers, greenery and ribbons.

The July 'demonstration' is presumably the same event as the Wool Fair, which was the opening event of the Chapel Wakes festivities each July. This occurred for almost 700 years until the final one was held in 1910. Here farmers were measured for suits to be produced from the wool of their own flocks.

To this day, some shepherds in the remoter areas of the High Peak use an archaic numbering system to count their sheep, a rare survival of the language of the ancient Celtic Britons. This system is also employed elsewhere in the north of England, in Cumbria and the Yorkshire Dales, each area having its own slightly different lingo. From one to twenty, the Derbyshire version runs:

Yain, Tain, Eddero, Pederro, Pitts, Tayter, Later, Overro, Coverro, Dix,
Yain-dix, Tain-dix, Eddero-dix, Peddero-dix, Bumfitt,
Yain-o-bumfitt, Tain-o-bumfitt, Eddero-o-bumfitt, Peddero-o-bumfitt, Jiggit

Why not give it a try next time you need to resort to counting sheep to get to sleep?

The American folklorist Charlotte Norman recorded the quaint tradition: 'It was the custom in the hill regions of Derbyshire when a shepherd died, to put a wisp of sheep wool under his chin so that when he met his maker, he would know him for a shepherd.'

Addy (1895) records a local superstition that has now presumably died out: 'There is a bone in a sheep's head, which is in shape somewhat like a cross, and is called "the lucky bone". In Derbyshire it is regarded as lucky to carry one of these bones in the pocket.'[96]

At Longshaw on the Sheffield–Derbyshire border, the annual Sheepdog Trials are held on the Thursday, Friday and Saturday of the first week of September. These are the longest-running sheepdog trials in the county, and are claimed as the earliest in England (earlier similar events having been held in

Trophies at Longshaw Sheepdog Trials.

New Zealand and Scotland). They are said to have arisen as a consequence of an argument at the Fox House Inn between shepherds and farmers as to who owned the best dog. After several years of informal trials between local farmers, the first official trial was held in 1898. A distinctive curiosity at the Longshaw trials is the time-keeping clock used to time the competitors, built in 1953. With a large clockface on the side of a shed, it resembles a giant version of those toy clocks that children learn to tell the time on. The programme invited any visitors inside to see the clock's inner workings, so being of a nosey nature, I took them up on the offer. Contained within was a Heath Robinson-style mechanism that whirred noisily, plus an assortment of spare car batteries to power it. The man stationed inside it told me, 'They could easily replace it with something modern and digital – but it's part of Longshaw heritage.'

Sheepdog Trials are also held at Bamford on Spring Bank Holiday, Dovedale in August, at Hope Show on August Bank Holiday Monday, at Chatsworth Country Fair in early September and at Little Hayfield Country Show in mid-September, where a sheep show in which various breeds are judged is also staged.

Buxton Museum has a display recreating the study of Victorian geologist and archaeologist Sir William Boyd Dawkins. Easily missed among the many treasures on display are a pair of mounted sheep's heads who stare down glassy-eyed at visitors from high up on the wall.

Behind these pieces of unassuming taxidermy is a remarkable tale of ovine derring-do. Back in 1830, a farmer from Rowlee Farm, Bamford, sold some of his flock of Penistone ewes at auction, which were bought by a farmer from Kent. Having been transplanted down south, two members of the flock decided that they couldn't hack soft southern ways and, apparently homesick for the bleak moorlands of the Peak District, elected to walk all the way back home, managing to successfully navigate their way cross-country to their original farm. Having staged this epic expedition, they were allowed by their former owner to live out their days in their home village. After they died, their heads were stuffed and mounted, and for many years hung on the wall in St Peter's Church, Hope, until some modernising vicar or churchwarden presumably thought them too ghoulish to be on display in a church. They were subsequently sent to Buxton Museum for safekeeping – at least they got to remain in their native High Peak.

At another St Peter's Church, the one at Edensor on the Chatsworth estate, an annual sheep service is held in spring with new-born lambs being blessed in the church.

In recognition of all this ovine heritage, 2016 saw the first Ashbourne Sheep Fair held in the town's Market Place, billed as 'A brand new event to promote sheep, sheep farmers, the products they produce and the hard work they do to the general public, there will be live music, CAMRA beer tent, wool spinners, [and] sheep shearing'. In 2019 the event organisers took the event over the county boundary into neighbouring Staffordshire and it was rebranded as the Uttoxeter Sheep Fair.

SHELDON DUCK TREE

In 1601 at the village of Sheldon near Bakewell a duck was observed flying into an ash tree but the bird did not re-emerge; the tree in question became known locally as the Sheldon Duck Tree, the story of the vanishing duck being passed down orally through the generations. The tree began to decay at the base of the trunk at the beginning of the twentieth century and subsequently had to be cut down as it was deemed it was becoming unsafe (its branches had grown to hang over the road through the village). Once it was chopped down, the timber was sold to the local joinery firm of Wilson & Son of Ashford in the Water.

When the joiners began to work the timber into planks, the perfect image of a cross-section of a duck was discovered within the grain of the wood. The boards were displayed at Ashford in the Water Post Office for a spell before being incorporated into a fireplace, and postcards of the duck image within the wood alongside a short accompanying text explaining the legend were produced by local stationer Ben Gratton of Bakewell. The text describes Sheldon dismissively as being 'noted for nothing in particular but the magnificent country which surrounds it and the difficulty of getting supplies up there during the long dreary winter'; although there again, given that a duck flying into a tree and disappearing was still a noteworthy local event that was being talked about 300 years down the line, perhaps the compiler of the text has a point.

SQUIRREL HUNTING

As a folklorist, I am normally inclined to lament the loss of an annual local custom. However, like the vast majority of people will be, I am glad to see the back of the more brutal ones – for example, the cock fighting, bull baiting and dancing bears that were once so popular at the Derbyshire Wakes Weeks. Under this category we can also file the traditional annual squirrel hunts that once took place across the county, occurring at Stanton-in-the-Peak in the Derbyshire Dales, Duffield in south Derbyshire and Cutthorpe in north-east Derbyshire.

While the squirrel hunts were an annual event, they all took place at different times of year in each locale. At Stanton the event occurred on Good Friday at Cowley Knoll, where great numbers of men and boys from surrounding villages assembled chanting 'Kill! Kill!' and attempted to shake squirrels out of the tree branches. Despite the chanting, the object was not actually to kill the squirrel – although presumably it was still a fairly terrifying ordeal for the creature.

At Duffield Wakes in early November a huge bonfire was constructed and then the following day, writes W. Henry Jewitt, a correspondent to Volume 14, No. 2 of *Folklore* journal, the local boys and young men visited Kedleston Park squirrel hunting: 'they used to take horns, old tea-trays, old cans, or any mortal thing which would make a horrid noise. Perhaps a hundred young fellows

The village of Stanton-in-the-Peak and surrounding countryside – formerly home to an annual Good Friday squirrel hunt.

thus provided would go under the trees in the park, where with their uproar some poor wretch of a squirrel would be so terrified that he would drop to the ground [...] What became of the poor wretch at last I do not know, I suppose he was killed.'[97]

Judith Stubbs, in her history of the village of Cutthorpe, reports that there the squirrel hunting occurred in the festive season and had a more practical underlying purpose: 'Squirrel hunting was generally practised at Christmas time and Christmas Pies were made from the meat.'[98]

In an article called 'Folk Dancing In Derbyshire' in one of the earliest volumes of *The Derbyshire Countryside* (the precursor to the glossy monthly of today, *Derbyshire Life*, which back then, as the organ of the Derbyshire Rural Community Council, dealt with altogether more rustic matters of county life), William J. Shipley of the Brampton Folk Dance Party (a kind of Derbyshire version of Cecil Sharp, Shipley collected and documented local folk songs, dance and drama performances) makes passing reference to a Morris dance named 'Hunting the Squirrel', although the connection, if any, to the former custom is unclear. In a strange incidence of cosmic connections, the folk song 'Hunt the Squirrel' is known to have been a favourite tune of professional musician and extraterrestrial communicator Philip Rodgers of Grindleford (QV).

TING TANG NIGHT

I came across reference to this obscure lost Derbyshire custom in a letter in the Dave Bathe archive kept at the University of Sheffield Library, and have not seen it recorded anywhere else. One of Bathe's respondents, Edith Spencer of Wirksworth, wrote in reply to his appeals in the local press for reminiscences from people who had witnessed Derbyshire guising performances in the early twentieth century. Spencer remembered visits from a guising troupe when she was a young girl, which frightened her at the time. As an aside, she continued:

> My main interest was in 'Ting-Tang' Night, the night of the 23rd [December], when the old custom was for men to walk the streets banging on anything that would make a loud noise, mainly tin cans, iron pots and spoons etc. which they did to frighten away evil so that the town would be ready to welcome the Christ Child. Up to the end of the last century this was undertaken annually, a procession of some importance apparently being formed. [...]
>
> My aunt told me of this custom, in which her brothers joined at one time. I believe the ditty was
>
> > Ting Tang Night
> > Stars are bright
> > Every little angel's
> > dressed in white.
>
> I understand that the custom gradually fell into disrepute.[99]

The custom sounds similar to one that still occurs annually in the Northamptonshire village of Broughton, where the villagers get together at midnight on the night of the first Sunday after 12 December to form the 'Broughton Tin Can Band', conducting a walk around the perimeter of the village and making as much noise as possible using anything that comes to hand (when I attended in 2012, the 'instrumentation' included drums, whistles, pots, pans and an antique hunting bugle). Nowadays no one really knows why this event takes place, with competing theories including (as at Wirksworth) to drive a generic 'evil' out of the village; to frighten away witches; to frighten away gypsies; a memorable bound-beating exercise to establish to the successive generations of village youth where the boundaries of the parish lay; or a hangover from a 'skimmington', 'Low-Belling' or 'Ran-tanning', where local wrongdoers were publicly exposed and punished (see Mob Justice).

Spencer goes on to suggest that Ting Tang Night could have been Wirksworth's very own localised version of Mischief Night, a particular night of the year on which children and youths were permitted to play extreme pranks, and that its rowdiness led to its downfall: 'Much drinking resulted in such pranks as gates being taken off hinges. Some called it "Mischief Night". I have been reliably told that Parliament passed a law forbidding such Mischief Nights (before the First World War) which it seems, were not confined to Wirksworth.'[100]

u

UNLOUSING

This is a lapsed Easter custom that was formerly practised in Derbyshire, also known under the various alternative names of 'Lifting', 'Cucking' or 'Heaving'; however, as I am otherwise struggling to come up with an entry to place under the letter 'U' in this *A–Z of Curious Derbyshire*, let's stick to calling it 'Unlousing'.

Writing in 1852 in an essay for *The Journal of the British Archaeological Association* on the 'Ancient Customs and Sports of the County of Derby', local antiquary Llewellynn Jewitt noted, 'On Easter Monday, the custom of lifting still obtains in some of the northern parts of the county', before describing the modus operandi:

> On this day the men lift the women, and the following day the women return the compliment. For this purpose, a chair, gaily decorated with ribbands, is carried from house to house by a number of young women, gaily dressed up for the occasion, and having caught some luckless fellow and placed him in the chair, they lift him above their heads three times. On being released from the chair, he receives a kiss from each of the women engaged in the ceremony, and in return presents them with some money.

By the twentieth century the social conventions seem to have shifted to the point where the custom was no longer viewed as a respectable one. Seth Evans in *Bradwell: Ancient and Modern*, published in 1912, observes that 'scores now living have taken part' in the custom, but concludes, 'the practice was not only vulgar, but sometimes positively indecent, and very properly died a natural death'.[101]

VANISHING VILLAGES

An old Derbyshire saying runs, 'When Chesterfield was gorse and broom, Leash Fen was a market town; Now Chesterfield's a market town, Leash Fen is but gorse and broom.'

The area now marked on maps as Leash Fen is a remote marshy spot on the moors between Chesterfield and Baslow. The legend highlights the fact that the settlements where we all live can exist on more precarious foundations than we might care (for the sake of our sanity) to dwell on. The formerly prosperous town of Leash Fen, or Leachfield, is said to have one day, without warning, sunk into the earth, the incident being witnessed by a solitary person stood nearby on higher ground. When drainage ditches were being dug across the moorland in the 1830s, fragments of earthenware pottery were found along with primitive coins and pieces of tool-cut oak that seem to have been poles to support wooden housing, giving a degree of credibility to the folk tale.

Derbyshire has over the years had several communities that for a variety of reasons have disappeared off the face of the map. In fact, there have been so many that a whole book has been devoted to this particular topic – Peter Naylor's *The Lost Villages of Derbyshire*.

The tiny village of Ballidon had only seventy-nine residents as of the 2001 census. It is recorded in Domesday Book (1086), but quarrying activity in the area over the years (the village falls conveniently *just* outside the boundary of the Peak District National Park) has reduced the settlement in size considerably. A relic of the village's former standing is All Saints Church, which dates to around 1205 but now finds itself marooned somewhat forlornly in the middle of a field and is under the care of the Friends of Friendless Churches charity.

Another abandoned church, complete with graveyard, can be found at Heath, near Chesterfield, in a little-known clearing close to the M1 motorway. The original Heath settlement seems to have been founded by Danish invaders in the late 800s, and Domesday Book records two separate hamlets of Lunt and Le Hethe in the vicinity of present-day Heath. By the mid-nineteenth century it

Somewhat forlorn and abandoned in a field: All Saints Church, Ballidon.

was decided to move the location of the village church, which dated from at least 1307, to the Lunt area, where most of the residents were by now living. All that now remains of this original church is part of the porch, with medieval incised stonework still visible.

The lost village of Hungry Bentley close to the similarly named Fenny Bentley (near Ashbourne) suggests to us that this community was unable to sustain itself owing to unsuitable conditions for growing crops, and hence was abandoned. In south Derbyshire, Barton Blount (which sounds rather like the name of a dashing gentleman spy character in an Ealing comedy) still exists as a tiny settlement of just seventy-four inhabitants as of the 2001 census, but the remains of a much larger medieval settlement including a chapel, duck decoy pond, substantial timber-framed building and open field system were excavated in the 1960s and '70s.

Another reason why a settlement could be lost was at the whim of the local aristocrat. The original estate village of Edensor was formerly located on the other side of the road to where it is now but was swept away by the Earl of Devonshire when building the current Chatsworth House so it wouldn't be visible from the so-called 'Palace of the Peak'. Similarly, when Kedleston Hall was being constructed, by Nathaniel Curzon in 1759, he decreed that the medieval village of Kedleston and public highway were resited beyond the boundaries of the Hall's parkland, retaining only the twelfth-century church of All Saints.

But vanished villages are by no means a phenomenon consigned to the annals of history. Derwent and Ashopton were a pair of sleepy Peak District villages nestled in the Derwent Valley, surrounded by rolling hills and within easy commuting distance of Sheffield. As is well-known, they were systematically emptied of residents, the buildings demolished and the valley artificially flooded in the 1940s in order to satisfy the growing household water requirements of the cities of Sheffield, Derby, Nottingham and Leicester, as well as the towns and villages under the care of Derbyshire County Council. This was the work of the Derwent Valley Water Board, incorporated in 1899 (later subsumed into the Severn Trent Water Authority). As the late local historian (and founder of the Derwent Dams Museum) Vic Hallam notes, 'When finished, the gains in water storage would be tremendous, but the loss of the beautiful and historic villages of Ashopton and Derwent would be a high price to pay.'[102]

The grandest house to be lost to the waters was Derwent Hall. Built in 1674 by Henry Balguy for his son as a wedding present, it changed hands between several local notables over the centuries, including a stint where it was used by the Duke of Norfolk as a shooting lodge. It was acquired by the Derwent Valley Water Board in 1927, and opened as a Youth Hostel in 1932. Upon closure, parts of the building were auctioned off, with the gates, steps and panelling all going off to various bidders. Captain J. St J. Balguy, a descendent of the family who initially built the hall, bought the lintel from above the doorway that bore the carved family crest. A sculpture from the stable block known as 'Peeping Tom' was relocated to Castleton Youth Hostel. The oak panelling from the hallway was bagged for the Mayor's Chamber of the new Council House that was being built at the time in Derby, nowadays the headquarters of Derby's Local Studies Library.

The village church, built in 1867 to replace various earlier places of worship on the site, did not even make its centenary. The Bishop of Derby preached the final sermon held at the church to a packed congregation on 17 March 1943, noting sadly, 'We build churches with the idea that they will endure forever, but we know in our hearts that our buildings will not endure, for we have seen so much destruction during the war that we no longer have the illusion of permanence of the work of human hands.'[103] As with the hall, the church effects were dispersed, with the silver and chalice going to Frecheville, the font ending up at Tansley, the east window going to Hathersage and the bells being installed at Chelmorton, near Buxton. The Water Board somewhat whimsically decided to leave the church spire standing after demolishing the rest of the church so it could be seen poking out of the water, an action that they later came to regret as its presence attracted numerous curious swimmers, and after an early dry period that lowered the level of the reservoir it was blown up in December 1947. As with many churches that ended up under water like those of Dunwich, the prosperous town in Suffolk destroyed by sea storms in the thirteenth century, a 'Legend of the Bells' grew up whereby folk tales spread that people visiting the area had heard the muffled ringing of church bells emanating from beneath the water.

The spire of Derwent Church is inspected by bystanders in the 1940s after the reservoir levels dropped.

Many of the villagers were rehomed at the small estate of houses built by the Water Board with the latest modern conveniences at Yorkshire Bridge just beyond the shores of Ladybower Reservoir. A more gruesome problem for the water corporation than what to do with the current living residents was where to rehome the 284 bodies buried in the village churchyard. Initially a piece of Water Board land at Yorkshire Bridge was set aside for their reinterment, and with the approval of the Bishop of Derby everything was close to being rubber-stamped, until it was realised that the law stated that no new burial grounds could be sited within a hundred yards of an existing dwelling house without the written consent of the owner of said property. There was only one house, Bamford Lodge, within 100 yards of the proposed new cemetery location, but the owner objected, sending the Water Board back to the drawing board. Finally, a mutual agreement between the Vicar of Bamford and the Water Board was reached whereby the Water Board paid to extend the existing graveyard at Bamford Church. A photograph shows tarpaulin sheets surrounding the church, behind which the grim task of opening the graves and labelling the contents in order that they could be reinterred in the correct spot at Bamford was taking place, under the supervision of the Derbyshire County Medical Officer.

Following the 2018 summer heatwave, by October and November the water level in the reservoir had dropped significantly and in sufficient quantity to reveal the remains of Derwent village once more. This aroused great interest from the general public – on my visit one November Sunday, half of the populations of Sheffield and Manchester seemed to be there picking over the exposed ruins. I overheard an elderly gentleman on the bus back to Sheffield telling a fellow passenger that for him it was a 'twice in a lifetime' experience to see what remained of Derwent again, having visited after the noteworthy 1976 heatwave.[104]

It was a surreal experience to find myself walking on what is usually the bottom of Ladybower Reservoir alongside large crowds of people coming together to explore the normally unseen ruins of Derwent. The semi-mythical story of Derbyshire's answer to Atlantis was something that clearly still held a powerful grip over the collective consciousness, despite presumably there being a vanishingly small amount of people remaining alive by 2018 who would have been able to recall the topography of the site before the creation of the reservoirs. There were families, dog walkers, cyclists, and an opportunistic metal detectorist present – I even saw a few babies being pushed in their prams along the muddy reservoir bed, as well as someone in a wheelchair.

When the reservoir level was low enough to reveal the foundations of the buildings of Derwent village in autumn 2018, the spectacle drew large crowds of people from the surrounding area to investigate.

Even the 1940s reservoir villages aren't the most recent example of a vanishing Derbyshire village. Growing up in the 1980s at South Darley, we used to visit my Auntie Mar in Bolsover most weekends. To get home we used to drive through Arkwright Town, which was on the left-hand side of the car as we made the return journey. But after 1988, it switched to the right-hand side, the reason being that following the closure of the local colliery, dangerous emissions of methane gas were discovered under the houses.

A native of Arkwright Town, Charles Dickens (not *that* Charles Dickens), born in 1940, remembers the original Arkwright Town as 'a close-knit, self-sufficient mining village which was mainly made up of five rows of terraced houses'.[105] Close-knit to the extent that Dickens reckoned he had been in every one of its 152 houses at some point. Such a close community ended up being self-policing, as Dickens remembered: 'When I was growing up in Arkwright you couldn't just wander off as you liked. Everybody knew everybody else, so any misdeeds were soon reported back, and then there'd be trouble.'[106] It had a public house (the Station Hotel), Miners' Welfare Club, five shops, a fish and chip shop, school, playing fields, allotments, youth club, chapel (later employed as a doctor's surgery) and, at one point, its own railway station. The builders of the replacement Arkwright strove to replicate this sense of a close community, retaining the former street names from the old village for the new estate that was built across the road.

WAKES WEEKS, MISHAPS AND TRAGEDIES

Many of Derbyshire's towns and villages hold annual carnivals in the summer months. However, a handful of locations style their yearly festivities as 'Wakes Weeks' – providing a link to a tradition dating back many centuries, to the early years of the adoption of Christianity in this country. The places in Derbyshire that still stage a Wakes Week in the twenty-first century are Tideswell, Hope, Parwich, Winster, Brassington, Kirk Ireton, Great Hucklow, Eyam and Hartington.

The Wakes began as a religious festival observed on the feast day of whichever saint the local church was dedicated to. People would remain awake and attend a service the night before with candles burning, conducting a night-time vigil to welcome in the saint's day. This custom is reflected in the torchlit evening procession still practised at the Wakes at Tideswell (using real flaming torches) and Hope (using battery-powered torches).

Over time the Wakes evolved to become a more secular and raucous affair – a key element being that the whole of the town or village shut down working operations together for the duration of the week and all residents holidayed together en masse. By the nineteenth century, Wakes Weeks seem to have become a phenomenon specific to northern England, with Lancashire mill towns often decanting to their county's coastline for the duration. In Derbyshire, however, the fun took place on the doorstep. They were not always traditionally a summer celebration – Melbourne, Birchover, Stoney Middleton and Taddington Wakes were all held in October, and Elton and Youlgrave Wakes took place in November.

The fun and frivolity was tempered by a sense of duty and industriousness, with the opportunity taken in the build-up to the festivities to clean and whitewash houses and cottages so the whole village would look at its best. Children were often clad in new outfits specially bought for the celebrations, and sometimes (as at Bonsall) the houses, shops and landmarks like the village cross were garlanded with flowers and evergreens.

TIDESWELL
WAKES & WELLDRESSING
JUNE 24 to JULY 2
Sheep Roast, Barrel Race, Carnival
Sports, Dancing, Torchlight Finale

Poster from around the 1960s advertising some of the events at the annual Tideswell Wakes Week.

'Tidza' (Tideswell) Wakes 2017.

The communal letting-off-steam frequently led to predictable results: old newspaper reports concerning Derbyshire Wakes Weeks are full of reports of drunken behaviour, affray, long-running grudges flaring up, smashed windows and brawling, with Bonsall Wakes frequently seeming a particular flashpoint – one Bonsall landlord admitted deliberately watering down his ale during Wakes Week.

The 1899 Wakes at Winster were livened up in an unexpected fashion – this report from the *Derbyshire Times* gives us a wonderful sense of the modern world coming crashing through into the olde-worlde streets of the village at this fin-de-siècle junction:

> This year the arrival of a motor car caused a sensation, as it was the first time a horseless carriage had been seen in the town [*sic*]. The occupants made their entry in very undignified fashion. Not being acquainted with the road, they came down the steep declivity known as Winster Bank [*sic* – Winster has two steep streets leading off from the Main Street, East Bank and West Bank] at a furious rate. The gentleman in charge lost control of the car, which ran into a trough at the reservoir. In jumping from the carriage, both the lady and gentleman were shaken. The car was left for alterations and repairs with the local blacksmith. [107]

With the Wakes being such a highly charged time, occasionally events could tip over into tragedy. At the 1892 Winster Wakes, 18-year-old Mary Bateman, daughter of a local farmer, was struck in the chest by a swing boat ride. She was unable to walk away from the scene of the accident and afterwards died from her injuries. Winster's local medic, Doctor Cantrell, conducted the inquiry and concluded the death resulted from concussion of the spine, recording the highly specific verdict, 'Died from injuries received by being knocked down by a swing boat.'

The *Belper News* of 2 July 1920 reported on the sad story of 26-year-old Samuel Davis, who attended Blackwell Wakes with his good friend Albert Neal, a blacksmith. The two lads had toured the various fairground rides and stalls together and decided to try their hand at the shooting gallery, competing as to who would prove the best marksman in shooting at celluloid balls suspended on water jets. While holding the gun, Neal turned sideways to respond to a remark made by Davis and the rifle discharged, the bullet striking Davis in the side of his head. He was taken to Chesterfield Hospital, where he subsequently died. Neal was unable to attend the inquest due to 'suffering from severe mental shock and would not be in a fit condition to give any evidence for the remainder of the

A donkey-riding Pierrot accompanied by brass band at Winster Wakes celebrations *c.*1910.

week' due to what had happened. Harry Scherdel, the dead man's half-brother, had seen Neal the day before the trial in bed and confirmed he was 'in a very rum way as a result of the occurrence'; Scherdel also offered his opinion that he 'considered [Neal] to be of a somewhat nervous disposition' in general.

The friends were reported to be very close and 'went about like two brothers'; the stallholder Ellen Mellors (who was said to have been in the travelling show business for twenty years and never had a similar incident happen on her rifle stall) reported that following the accident Neal 'picked [Davis] up, kissed him, and cuddled him until the arrival of the doctor'. A verdict of accidental death was reached.

WELL DRESSINGS (CONTROVERSIAL)

Well dressing is a local tradition of ancient origin whose fame justly spreads well beyond the confines of the county. Every year throughout the summer months, teams of volunteers at sites across Derbyshire work tirelessly to produce elaborate pictorial designs using only flower petals and other natural materials pressed into large boards filled with clay to give thanks for the essential gift of water.

Observing the coachloads of Darby and Joan Club members pouring into Tissington on Ascension Day, who go forth to admire the wells and gorge on cream teas, you would be hard pressed to find a more twee scene of English rural life. And yet a comb through the annals of history tells a different – and more unlikely – story: well dressings have proved more controversial than the Turner Prize over the years.

A big source of aggravation in the past was the drunken behaviour of attendees of the well dressings and the stalls and attractions that pitched up around the annual floral displays. The *Buxton Advertiser* reporter of 4 June 1870 recommended in somewhat hysterical fashion that Buxtonians avoid their own well dressings (begun in 1840 when the Duke of Devonshire provided a public water supply) and visit the ones at Tissington instead for a simpler and more authentic experience:

> What a relief and pleasure it was after the dust and turmoil of the previous Thursday at Buxton. No shouting showmen and crashing drums and trumpets […] It is pleasant to contrast what was seen at Tissington with what was experienced at Buxton. The pleasing half religious celebration at one place with the coarseness and brutality which prevailed and obscured the prettier features of the other. At Tissington it is a work of love maintained by the affections of generations. At the other place it is a Saturnalia kept up for the most sordid of purposes and unredeemed by the slightest poetry […] Without either clergy or a Lord of the Manor to give a tone to the affair and prevent it sinking into the lowest orgies, and without the local authorities trying to prevent an influx of characters from surrounding towns to poison and degrade, the well flowering here has fallen justly into disrepute.

Despite the local paper's misgivings, the well dressings remained popular with the townsfolk, but the organisation of the event floundered around the turn of the century. The *Ashbourne Telegraph* reported in 1904 that, 'At a meeting at Buxton on Friday night, convened for the purpose of deciding whether the ancient custom of well-dressing should be resuscitated, four persons only turned up, and these passed a resolution that there should be no well-dressing this year. Their action is being freely criticised.' In 1908 the council tried to push for the well dressing to be held in Whit week, a suggestion that was unpopular with local shopkeepers and businesspeople. Matters came to a head when a party led by a Mr Sturgess hastily erected an unofficial well dressing

'In Defence of an Old Custom': the 1908 Buxton well dressing design that almost sparked a riot.

in protest at the council dragging their heels, bearing the pointed motto, 'In Defence of an Old Custom'. The *Sheffield Telegraph* reported in their 16 July edition the events that followed under the startling headline 'Buxton Sensation – Council and People in Conflict – Almost a Riot':

> The Market Place at Buxton presented a riotous scene at noon to-day, the officials of the District Council and the people coming into conflict. Last night the Higher Buxton well was dressed by the upholders of the ancient custom. This morning the Council met hurriedly, and resolved that it be undressed. Mr Grieve, Town Surveyor, and officials, proceeded to carry out the resolution. One man carried a big pair of shears, and another a knife, but the news had reached Mr Sturgess, the principal promoter, and he and a crowd of working-men defended the well. The police came, and 2,000 people flocked to the scene. Everybody was bustled, and a few people were slightly injured. Mr Sturgess defied the authority of the council, and but for Supt. James an open riot would have taken place.

People power!

The local constabulary must have come to dread it when the annual well dressing time came around again, and none more so than the unfortunate PC Rupert Leese who, the *Derbyshire Courier* of 11 September 1858 reported, was called in on three occasions by local landlords to disturbances at pubs during the Chelmorton well dressing on 19 August. On one of these visits Leese encountered James Wardle, who tore 'the constable's trousers all to pieces'. At his subsequent court appearance Wardle was fined '10s, expenses 13s 6d, with a caution, and also 14s for a pair of new trousers'.[108] Giving evidence to the court, a Superintendent McKenzie noted that 'it was a matter of notoriety that defendant and his family were in the habit going up and down the country to raise rows and clear public-houses'.[109]

It is generally believed that the decorating of wells with greenery is an ancient custom pre-dating Christianity, when our nature-revering pagan ancestors worshipped stones, trees and springs. As with many elements of pagan worship, the early Christian Church assimilated conventions of the earlier religions – including the veneration of wells and springs, which were reborn as holy wells, which is why you will see the majority of Derbyshire's well dressings being blessed by the local vicar when they first go up. The relationship with the Church hasn't always been smooth, however. In Derby, St Alkmund's Well was dressed from the 1850s onwards. Crichton Porteous in *The Beauty and Mystery of Well Dressing* notes, 'This seems to have been continued till in 1919 the Rev. John Steel Wilding became vicar. By then, he said, the ceremony had become mainly an excuse for many persons getting drunk, and the blessing and dressing of the well were stopped.'[110]

These ideological tussles continued into modern times. In Eyam in 2006 one of the well dressing designs depicted the Green Man, a pagan emblem of a male face sprouting greenery. The Rector of Eyam at the time, Reverend Andrew Montgomerie, blessed the village's other two designs as normal, but felt unable to perform the ceremony at the Town End well with the Green Man design. He told the *Derbyshire Times*: 'To me this is a pagan symbol. As a Christian I see it as an inappropriate subject matter and I cannot be expected to bless it – I can't simply brush my beliefs under the carpet to keep people happy.'

Montgomerie's stance caused quite a stir in the village and a local resident remembers villagers dressing up in Green Man costumes for the Wakes Week fancy dress parade that marks the end of the wells dressing week, as a satirical comment on the hoo-hah.

The 1960s: the times they were a-changin'. The massive social upheavals and cultural shifts of the decade even penetrated the genteel world of Derbyshire village well dressing. A couple of controversial designs in that decade made the pages of the national press. At Wirksworth, a stark comment on the Cold War and CND movement was made by a 1960 well dressing design showing a pair of children witnessing the detonation of a nuclear bomb. The *Daily Express* reported on a well dressing design from nearby Bonsall in 1961 that showed 'Christ in modern dress, standing before a jack-booted Gestapo officer and guarded by a steel-helmeted soldier armed with a sub-machine gun'. The design won the first prize that year but was said to have shocked some of the older well dressers of the village, one of whom called it 'a mockery and a travesty of the ancient custom of well dressing'. This design seems to have set the ball rolling, as in the following years Peggy Blodwell (Bonsall's answer to Tracey Emin) produced a succession of designs that caused a stir with themes including adultery, devils prancing on bishops to represent the apathy of the Church, and anti-Apartheid. The village vicar, the Reverend Laurence Wood, assured the outside world that while these tableaux had all provoked debate locally, there was no sense of disharmony: 'We are a happy little village and I didn't want it to be divided by controversy that was brought on by other people. There has never been an argument in the village about the well.'

Well dressings retain their unlikely power to cause controversy into the twenty-first century. During the strange Covid summer of 2020, the Youlgrave Well Dressing Committee took the decision to modify how the dressings were produced, to maintain the tradition throughout the uncertain times of the pandemic while safely adhering to the social distancing regulations that remained in place to try to slow the spread of the virus. Accordingly, instead of the large panels that are normally dressed by teams of volunteers working together in a confined space, a series of small-scale panels were constructed to enable participants to design and produce their own designs individually.

In addition to the pandemic that was raging across the globe, another incident in the febrile summer of 2020 that had worldwide repercussions was the death in Minneapolis on 25 May of George Floyd, an African American man who was killed by a police officer using brutally heavy-handed methods while attempting to arrest him. This incident proved the tipping point that sparked a huge outcry against institutional racism and consequent public protests worldwide.

Tim Walton-Pearce was inspired by the events in the news to design a small well dressing board bearing the motto 'Black Lives Matter' against a black backdrop. Unfortunately, shortly after the twenty or so individual boards went up on display on 20 June on the steps of the 'Fountain' (the central stone water tank dated 1829 when Youlgrave got its first supply of piped water), a bystander obviously took exception to the messaging of this particular dressing and stole the board in protest. The board, minus its contents, was subsequently found at the side of a road further down the village.

However, perhaps the most infamous well dressing controversy of recent times erupted in 2017 when the team who produce the well dressing at the pump in Chesterfield Market Place chose for their theme a design depicting Princess Diana, marking both the twenty-year anniversary of her death in a Paris car crash and the fact that a recently married Diana had visited Chesterfield to officially open The Pavements shopping complex in 1981.

It is notoriously difficult to recreate the human face through the medium of well dressing, but the dressers of Chesterfield gamely gave it their best shot. Their heartfelt tribute unfortunately came out a little … wonky, and the well dressing quickly went viral, with images being shared across the world over the internet and everyone and their auntie wading in to offer their opinion online as to the artistry.

Many people thought the design better resembled other celebrities than Diana, with suggestions ranging from Worzel Gummidge, Alan Partridge, Theresa May, Thom Yorke in a wig, and Rod Stewart to Clare Balding. Thomas Hunt observed, 'It looks like a cross between Bonnie Tyler, a hedgehog and Janet Street Porter.'

An American lady commenting on the story being reported on the website royalcentral.co.uk felt with conviction she had uncovered the true motives of the Chesterfield well dressers: 'That flower display is not "art". It is a horrible site set up by Camilla supporters who are showing how they think Diana should be portrayed to anger people who liked Diana and loathe Camilla.'

The following year as usual, I went along to document the making of the well dressing, and was walking through the Pavements thinking what approach I could tactfully use to draw comment on the previous year's fiasco from the well dressing team – what would Louis Theroux say in this situation? Finally the answer for the perfect opener came to me, and I sidled up to one of the dressers and said, 'It's good to see that you are still making one after what happened last year.' 'Well,' came the reply through gritted teeth, 'we've been making them for the past thirty years so we're not about to stop now.'

Over at the Crooked Spire, the team producing the dressing displayed in the porch were both simultaneously miffed that their efforts the previous year had been totally overlooked in the glare of the media storm, while also relieved that their design had not been subject to such public scrutiny: 'I should have died if that happened to us,' one of them remarked.

Left: Chesterfield's controversial well dressing tribute to Princess Diana in 2017.

Below: Channel 5 News crew gathering opinion from locals about the Princess Diana well dressing.

They were also doing their diplomatic best to avoid being drawn into criticising the work of the team across town, although one team member was eventually moved to concede: 'It were the lips that were the problem … she was a very beautiful lady in real life.'

THE 'WILD MAN' OF BAKEWELL

Edwardian local newspaper journalists had a knack for knowing how to reel you into a story.

Under the heading 'Bakewell's 'Wild Man' – Mysterious Open-Air Bathing', the *Sheffield Telegraph*'s correspondent in the 3 May 1904 edition dramatically set the scene on recent events that had caused a stir in the Peakland town: 'Bakewell, famous for its church, its proximity to Haddon Hall, its puddings, and other historical associations, is in the grip of a modern sensation. It is troubled, and its mind is not at rest.'[111]

The paper reported how the preceding Sunday had seen hundreds of people descend on Wicksop Wood in the hope of getting a glimpse of a mysterious male who, judging by his appearance, could almost have been transplanted to Edwardian Bakewell from the prehistoric age.

The first sighting of this unusual character came on Friday, 29 April. Just below Wicksop Wood can be found Bakewell Golf Course, and it was here that several young lady members were playing an innocuous round of golf when they were startled by 'the apparition of a man, whose clothes were invisible' as the newspaper correspondent quaintly puts it.

The figure unexpectedly leapt over the boundary wall separating the golf club from the neighbouring woods, but upon seeing the group of ladies he swiftly retreated back into the trees. The ladies made a complaint and Bakewell's finest in the shape of Inspector Payne was dispatched into the woodland to investigate.

Whilst vagrants are not traditionally noted for their attention to personal hygiene, Bakewell's Wild Man appeared to buck this trend – Payne was unable to find any trace of the fellow in the woods, but concluded, 'Near the spot where the man appeared is a small pond, which suggested that he might have been enjoying an open-air bathe, and running about to dry himself.' His colleague, Superintendent Lakin, was 'inclined to the opinion that the mysterious stranger may simply be a visitor in Bakewell, who is fond of open-air bathing. But he admits that three baths a day are above the average.'

As the newspaper correspondent notes, in small rural towns any out of the ordinary happening soon becomes widely known: 'News soon spreads, and this remarkable affair was the talk of Bakewell in a very short time. Then other facts came to light, which confirmed the story and increased the mystery.'

Two further sightings were reported, all from locations near water (which prompted Lakin's comment above about the three baths in a day). Firstly, a young local farmer named Herbert Littlewood came forward to report that the same afternoon he had been in a plantation by the riverside and had also seen the same character, and had been unsure on whether to challenge him about his behaviour. Littlewood described the mystery stranger as 'a tall man, between 25 and 30 years of age'.

A third sighting from later the same day of a man 'in a state which suggested bathing was his object' (another convolutedly coy Edwardian euphemism for starkers) came in from Fillyfoot Bridge, near Rowsley.

News of the Wild Man's appearance captivated imaginations far beyond Bakewell, with syndicated reports of his naked antics appearing in regional newspapers across all corners of the UK, including the *Bicester Herald*, *Tyrone Courier*, *Exmouth Journal* and *Diss Express*.

The *Derby Daily Telegraph* of 6 May 1904 provides us with a tentative conclusion to the mystery of Bakewell's Wild Man, reporting that a 34-year-old ex-schoolmaster named Edward John Raynes, formerly a resident of the West Yorkshire town of Keighley but more recently residing at the Cheddleton Asylum, Leek, had been arrested in Keighley. Under questioning, Raynes admitted to have recently passed through Bakewell, although how he arrived at Keighley was said to be 'still a mystery'.

If Raynes and Bakewell's Wild Man were indeed one and the same, his appearance in Keighley was slightly more decent – while still deviating from societal norms: 'He wore a handkerchief on his head in place of a hat, and his clothes were very dirty. He attracted attention by scattering grains of wheat as he went along the street.'

The paper concluded, 'The story of Raynes is a sad one. It is stated that he applied himself to study with such assiduity that his mind gave way while he was preparing to take his M.A. degree.' The moral of the story: don't think about things too much or try too hard, otherwise you might find yourself naked on a golf course in Bakewell ...

X

X-RATED MATERIAL

If you enter a particular building in the Derbyshire village of Brassington and look upwards, you will be greeted by a shockingly obscene sight – a naked and very obviously male figure with dangling genitalia, deliberately pulling apart his buttocks to reveal his anus while peering over his shoulder and leering at you. What a charming welcome!

The 'mooning' male figure in St James' Church, Brassington.

A gargoyle pleasuring himself on the exterior of St Peter's Church, Hope.

What makes the presence of this obscene figure all the more shocking is that the building in question is not a brothel, sex shop or the kind of specialist cinema normally found in the backstreets of Soho, but the village church, dedicated to St James, which dates back to the Norman era.

The Brassington 'mooner' is a stone carving of clearly a very great age. But what is he doing here? The church guidebook merely notes wearily that the carving 'suggests that our medieval forbears were more broad-minded than us about what is suitable decoration for a church'.[112]

The same can be said for another male gargoyle figure on the exterior of St Peter's Church, Hope, engaged in the act of pleasuring himself. With one hand he appears to be tugging at his cheek and with the other hand tugging at ... another part of his body.

Female counterparts to the Brassington and Hope figures are even more plentiful across Derbyshire. At the ancient church of St Helen, Churchtown, Darley Dale is to be found a Sheela na gig, a weathered stylised carving of a crude female figure exposing her vulva.

Nearby at Haddon Hall, a large Sheela na gig carving is sited inside the former stable block that now houses a restaurant and toilets – formerly it was located on the exterior wall over the door, but it has been resited to prevent weathering damage. This Sheela is unique in that it is the only example of such a carving in Britain located in a non-church setting. Rumour has it that the carving was found buried in a nearby field, although as the Sheela na gig Project website explains, concrete evidence to back up this claim is rather shaky:

According to one of the guides at Haddon Hall the sheela was found in a field nearby and is much older than the hall itself but he also admitted to not knowing that much about the sheela so we have to take that with a pinch of salt. The 'found in field' origin for the Sheela may be related to a roman altar to Mars which stands just inside the great hall. This apparently was dug up in one of the fields.[113]

At Alderwasly, an alleged Sheela na gig carved from sandstone is sited on the exterior wall of a building formerly used as a chapel, which now houses the village hall after a period of lying derelict. Weathering over the years has made the features of the figure indistinct and therefore the jury is out as to whether this can be counted as an example of a Sheela na gig or not.

In recent years a couple of new Derbyshire Sheela na gigs have been uncovered. At an undetermined point in the 2000s, a large free-standing carved slab of gritstone bearing a Sheela na gig figure was uncovered during building work on a path at Church Street in Ashbourne (a stone slab's throw from the town's church of St Oswald, dating from 1240 and located on the site of an earlier Saxon church, therefore highly likely to be the place of origin of the sculpture). This remarkable carving of a skeleton-like figure was originally thrown into a skip alongside other rubble from the building work but fortunately its value was realised before the skip was emptied, and it now lies in the private hands of a local collector.

In 2020 an additional newly discovered Sheela na gig figure carved on the font of the defunct church of All Saints, Ballidon (see Vanished Villages), was reported to the Sheela na gig Project website.

The Haddon Hall Sheela na gig carving located in the stable block.

YOLGREFF/YOELGREVE/YOLEG (... ETC.)

What's in a name? Several locations in Derbyshire seem unable to agree on how to spell their own names, including Mappleton (also spelt Mapleton) on the Derbyshire–Staffordshire border (the location since the early 1980s of an unusual New Year's Day tradition, the Mappleton/Mapleton Bridge Jump, where participants leap off the parapet of Okeover Bridge and into the chilly River Dove below), and the tiny hamlet near Matlock where I grew up, Oaker.

We always deployed the 'a' during the first twelve years of my life when we were living there, and are backed up on this by the Ordnance Survey (although somewhat confusingly, there is also an 'Oker Road' and 'Oker Farm' marked on the map). Contrary to what many locals think, the 'oak' in Oaker does not refer to Will Shore's Tree, the prominent tree on the brow of Oaker Hill (which is a sycamore, not an oak). Romans were active in this area (their coins and remains of lead smelting equipment have been found locally) and named it in Latin 'Occursus', or the 'Hill of Conflict' – leading to the belief that a military fort was strategically sited here on the high ground.

But the confusing name capital of Derbyshire is surely the village of Youlgrave, near Bakewell.

Nowadays the most common dilemma for anyone attempting to write out the name of the village is whether or not to drop an 'e', as it appears on modern road signs as both 'Youlgrave' and 'Youlgreave'; the majority of local residents opt for the spelling minus the superfluous 'e', however, so that is the spelling I have opted for whenever referring to Youlgrave throughout the text of this book, as it feels like it has the greatest ring of authenticity. A road sign at Newhaven to the south-west of the village gets totally confused and hedges its bets by employing three 'e's, running with the frankly preposterous 'Youlegreave'.

In Domesday Book, the village makes an appearance under the name of Giolgrave. Research conducted by the late Bill Shimwell,[114] a former village resident, local historian and schoolteacher, has uncovered that over sixty different spellings of the village name have been employed over the years:

The Mappleton (or is it Mapleton?) Bridge Jump.

Giolgrave, Yolgrave, Jalgrave, Hyolgrave, Hyolegrave, Yolgreff, Yoleg, Yolegreve, Yolegrave, Youlgraue, Welegreve, Yoelgreve, Oelgreve, Yelegreve, Yeolegreve, Yolgreave, Yolgreve, Yollegreve, Jol've, Zolgrelf, Yollgreve, Yoligrewe, Yollegrewe, Youlgreve, Zolgreff, Youlgrave, Yolgreyva, Yolgreyve, Yeolgreave, Youlgreave, Yellegrave, Yollogreve, Yollograve, Yeollgreave, Youldgreave, Yograve, Isgrave, Yalgrove, Yolegreue, Jolegreue, Iolegrave, Jholegreve, Yelegrave, Yellegrave, Iolgrave, Yholgreve, Yelgreve, Zolgreve

According to Shimwell's findings, today's frontrunners first put in an appearance in 1492 (Youlgrave) and 1595 (Youlgreave).

C Minus, Must Try Harder: a road sign bearing directions to 'Youlegreave' [sic] at Newhaven.

The village website posits that:

> Although the name is sometimes translated as grove of Iola (or Geola) the clearest connection is with lead mining, which has been carried out in the limestone hills of the Peak District since Roman times. A grove or groove is an old term for a mine or open workings (miners were often known as groovers); and it is likely that the village name derives from 'yellow grove', the yellow probably referring to a colour found in the local rock (possibly baryte or barium sulphate).[115]

Lead mining remained an important part of the economy into the twentieth century – with tragic consequences on 23 May 1932 when a huge underground explosion at the Mawstone Mine just outside the village killed eight local men.

One way village residents (and those of nearby communities) get around all this spelling confusion entirely is to refer to Youlgrave by its popular nickname, 'Pommie'. This is thought to have originated from existence of the long-running village band (originally a brass band but nowadays a silver band) who can still be found out in force providing a rousing musical accompaniment during the blessing of the village well dressings ceremony in late June. When originally formed with instruments supplied by the local Co-operative stores (housed in an elegant building now forming the premises of a YHA youth hostel), the original members' lack of proficiency was said to be such that anything they attempted to play came out as a generic 'pom, pom, pom' kind of sound.

Z

ZOO

The north-east Derbyshire village of Ashover was described by a Victorian guidebook as having 'its own special charm of colour and character',[116] and in a collection of oral history reminiscences of older villagers gathered in the early twenty-first century as follows:

> It contained, in the early part of the twentieth century, around 3,000 people in a compact village centre surrounded by a number of outlying farmsteads and hamlets. A working community with quarrying and farming providing the main employment, its geographical position, within a ring of hills, encouraged self-sufficiency and created a village of unique character. [...] Although it is relatively near the large cities of Sheffield and Nottingham and the towns of Chesterfield and Matlock are but a few miles away, Ashover retains, even now, an 'away from it all' feeling. Within living memory it was positively remote, so that a person who originated in the neighbouring parish of Matlock was not considered to be 'a local' when he moved into the village.[117]

Despite this sense of remoteness, during the middle years of the twentieth century Ashover was home to a tourist attraction of sorts, in the form of a small zoo given the rather florid name 'Pan's Garden'. The zoo was the brainchild of married couple Clinton and Jill Keeling, who according to most accounts of their home life were perpetually at war with one another, and administered from their house and gardens at Hill Top House.

One star attraction at the zoo was the 'Sugar Puffs Bear', a precursor to the Honey Monster (who first put in an appearance in 1977), who helped to promote the sugary cereal in television adverts. Like many who are thrust into the spotlight, the pressure of sudden fame seems to have become all too much for Ashover's Sugar Puffs Bear, as on one occasion he escaped from his cage at the zoo and went on the run through the north-east Derbyshire countryside, before being spotted and recaptured by a quick-thinking local farmhand.

Someone who would go on to be one of Pan's Garden's fiercest critics in print was actually born on the premises in October 1956 – Clinton and Jill's son Jeremy, who shared the living space in the two-bedroom cottage with his parents, three siblings, 'seven dogs, a parrot, a chimp, a Senegalese bushbaby, a slow loris, various reptiles and, in a room to itself, a puma'.[118] In his autobiography *Jeremy and Amy* he recalls, 'Looking back it amazes me how dangerous it was to visit our zoo in those days before healthy [*sic*] and safety was invented. A large number of our enclosures, housing animals such as monkeys, otters, seals and vultures, had no safety barriers to protect visitors from being injured or even maimed.'[119] Thankfully nothing quite so dramatic occurred during the zoo's tenure – but some of the monkeys and parrots did develop a taste for kleptomania, pilfering everything from visitors' wedding rings to false teeth ...

Despite these unpromising beginnings, Jeremey Keeling would grow up to co-found the successful conservation charity Monkey World down in Dorset – a very different breed of zoo to Pan's Garden.

Richard Bradley was born in Sheffield in 1980 and raised at Oaker and Two Dales, near Matlock. Since 2014 he has been travelling Derbyshire and the Peak District researching and documenting the customs, traditions and folklore of the area and has been a monthly feature writer for *Derbyshire Life* magazine since July 2020. He has also written for titles including *Record Collector, Best of British* and *Picture Postcard Monthly*. His photographs have appeared in titles including *The Guardian, Daily Express, Sunday Times, Financial Times, Farmers Guardian* and *Discover Britain* magazine. In 2019 he held an exhibition 'Weird Derbyshire and Peakland' at Buxton Museum and Art Gallery, where a selection of his photographs of local customs were displayed alongside items from the Museum's reserve collections that are not normally on display. *The A–Z of Curious Derbyshire* is his fourth local history book after *Secret Chesterfield, Secret Matlock and Matlock Bath* and *Chesterfield in 50 Buildings*.

Endnotes

1 Brushfield, T., 'Reminiscences of Ashford-in-the-water, Sixty Years Ago', *The Reliquary* Vol. 6 (1865–66), p.14.

2 Uttley, Alison, *The Button-Box and Other Essays* (London: Faber and Faber, 1968), p.24.

3 University of Sheffield, Dave Bathe Collection, ACT/97-003/2/2/4, Spiral-bound notebook containing DB's ms. notes on […] local Winster supernatural beliefs and legends from Alan Stone.

4 peaklandheritage.org.uk/index.asp?peakkey=41200321, accessed 1 May 2016. Note the various spellings of the farm, which I have variously seen given as Gurdhall, Gurdall, Gurdale and Gird Hall.

5 Pers. comm. with author, 2 May 2018.

6 *Glossop Record*, Saturday, 4 February 1860, p.3.

7 *Derbyshire Advertiser and Journal*, Friday, 11 October 1878, p.3.

8 *Chester Courant*, Tuesday, 5 June 1821, p.4.

9 *Morning Post*, Thursday, 16 August 1821, p.2.

10 Ibid.

11 Hannant, Sara, *Mummers, Maypoles and Milkmaids: A Journey Through the English Ritual Year* (London: Merrell, 2011), p.72.

12 www.facebook.com/groups/6756582437746912/posts/6954714514600369, post by Chris Downings to 'Buxton 'Spatown' & District Photographs' Facebook page, 5 February 2022.

13 www.ancestry.co.uk/genealogy/records/anne-kendall-24-1bxjqv, accessed 13 July 2022.

14 Jewitt, Llewellynn, *The Ballads & Songs of Derbyshire* (London: Bemrose & Lothian, 1867), p.115.

15 *Derbyshire Times*, Saturday, 2 January 1869, p.3.

16 traditionalcustomsand ceremonies.com/2015/12/31/custom-revived-harthills-derby-tup, accessed 27 December 2021.

17 Drury, Jim, *'Fetch The Juicy Jam!' and other Memories of Birchover* (Birchover: The Reading Room, 2001), p.47.

18 *Derbyshire Times and Chesterfield Herald*, Friday, 17 May 1935, p.7.

19 Ibid.

20 Ibid.

21 *Derby Daily Telegraph*, Friday, 26 May 1905, p.2.

22 *Sheffield Daily Telegraph*, Tuesday, 30 May 1905, p.5.

23 'Town and County Gossip', *Derby Daily Telegraph*, Monday, 14 September 1908, p.2.

24 Ibid.

25 Maypole Promotions, *Milford and Makeney Milestones* (Milford: Maypole Promotions, 2002), p.43.

26 'Twilight of the English Celts', *Chronicle*, BBC2, TX date 27 October 1977.

27 Ratcliffe, Thomas, contribution to Andrews, Alexander (ed.), *Long Ago: A Journal of Popular Antiquities*, Vol. 1, (London: F. Arnold, 1873), p.350. Accessed online (31 July 2022) at archive.org/details/longago00unkngoog/page/n350

28 In this account, Ratcliffe does not mention the particular villages or even general area (beyond 'Derbyshire') he is reminiscing about; however, he was a frequent contributor on local customs and folklore to local newspapers and Notes and Queries columns, where he gives his place of origin as Coxbench.

29 Ratcliffe, Thomas, contribution to Andrews, Alexander (ed.), *Long Ago: A Journal of Popular Antiquities*, Vol. 1, (London: F. Arnold, 1873) p.350. Accessed online (3 December 2019) at archive.org/details/longago00unkngoog/page/n350

30 Ibid.

31 Walker, W., *A History of Tideswell Including the Surrounding Villages* (Tideswell: W. Walker, 1951), p.21.

32 Moore Smith, G.C., 'Bonfire night', *Notes and Queries*, Vol. s12-V, Issue 99 (December 1919), p.318; 'Brimington' has been mis-spelt as 'Birmigton'.

33 Severn, Joseph Millot, *My Village: Owd Codnor, Derbyshire, and the Village Folk when I Was a Boy* (Brighton: Joseph M. Severn, 1935), pp.94–95.

34 Goss, William Henry, *The Life and Death of Llewellynn Jewitt* (London: Henry Gray, 1889), p.227.

35 *Derbyshire Times*, Saturday, 15 December 1883, p.6.

36 www.greatbritishlife.co.uk/things-to-do/whats-on/the-hen-racing-world-championships-in-bonsall-6499874, accessed 29 July 2022.

37 Drury, Jim, *'Fetch The Juicy Jam!' and other Memories of Birchover* (Birchover: The Reading Room, 2001), p.14.

38 Brindley, Frank H., 'They laid the ghost of a mad dog', *The Nottinghamshire Guardian*, Saturday, 6 June 1953, p.5.

39 Ibid.

40 Ibid.
41 Ibid.
42 Ibid.
43 Ibid.
44 Ibid.
45 Ibid.
46 Ibid.

47 Miles, Clement A., *Christmas in Ritual and Tradition: Christian and Pagan* (London: Fisher Unwin, 1912), p.274.

48 University of Sheffield, Dave Bathe Collection, ACT/97-003/1/1/192, Hilda Shepherd letter, 4 February 1983.

49 'Cost of a Kiss at Troway', *Derbyshire Times and Chesterfield Herald*, Saturday, 21 January 1871, p.6.

50 Quoted in Charlton, Christopher and Buxton, Doreen, *Matlock Bath: A Perfectly Romantic Place* (Matlock: Derwent Valley Mills World Heritage Site Educational Trust, 2019), p.212.

51 Lawrence, Ada & Gelder, G. Stuart, *Early Life of D.H. Lawrence: Together with Hitherto Unpublished Letters and Articles* (London: Martin Secker, 1932).

52 Quoted from woodlandschapel. wordpress.com/alport-love-feast, accessed 31 July 2022.

53 *Nottinghamshire Guardian*, Friday, 2 November 1883, p.12.

54 Ibid.

55 *Derbyshire Courier*, Tuesday, 24 May 1910, p.4.

56 www.rightmove.co.uk/house-prices/baslow.html, accessed 30 March 2022.

57 Severn, Joseph Millot, *My Village: Owd Codnor, Derbyshire, and the Village Folk when I Was a Boy* (Brighton: Joseph M. Severn, 1935), pp.43.

58 Haywood, Barbara, *A Rake Through The Past: Memories of Middleton-by-Wirksworth*, (Cromford: Barbara Haywood, 1996), p.11.

59 Ibid.

60 *Derbyshire Courier*, Tuesday, 8

September 1885, p3.

61 Ibid.

62 Ibid.

63 *Sheffield Independent*, Monday, 7 October 1889, p.3.

64 Addy, Sidney Oldall, *Household tales with other traditional remains collected in the counties of York, Lincoln, Derby and Nottingham* (London: David Nutt, 1895), p.76.

65 Ibid.

66 Ibid.

67 *Ashbourne Telegraph*, Friday, 9 September 1904, p.12.

68 www.derbytelegraph.co.uk/burton/naked-man-said-took-clothes-3501442, accessed 1 July 2022.

69 Ibid.

70 Ibid.

71 Flamsteed, John, 'Memoirs of Mr. John Flamsteed, by Himself' in Wright, Raymond, *Old stories and writings about Derbyshire: Culled from various almost forgotten sources and authors and put together for the first time in the hope that they will be thus preserved from oblivion.* (Buxton: Borough of Buxton Public Library, 1933).

72 Shipley, William J., 'Folk Dancing In Derbyshire', *The Derbyshire Countryside* Vol. 1 No. 4 (Oct 1931), p.64.

73 University of Sheffield, Dave Bathe Collection, ACT/97-003/1/2/3, Dave Bathe's notebook.

74 Ibid.

75 Ibid.

76 Connole, Nellie, *Dark at Seven – The Life of a Derbyshire Miner: Being an account of his life as told by Joseph Sharpe of Coal Aston in the County of Derbyshire, 1859–1936* (York: Whitehead Books, 1988), p.27.

77 Ibid.

78 Ibid, pp.28–29.

79 University of Sheffield, Dave Bathe

Collection, ACT/97-003/1/1/184, Mrs. C. Ralphs letter, 14 December 1982.

80 Firth, J.B., *Highways and Byways in Derbyshire* (London: Macmillan and Co., 1908 (First Edition 1905)), p.350.

81 Quoted in www.greatbritishlife.co.uk/homes-and-gardens/places-to-live/quarndon-s-fascinating-spa-resort-past-6512442, accessed 29 July 2022.

82 Ramsbottom, Laurence, 'Folk Stories of Peakland', in *National Association of Head Teachers Conference Souvenir, Buxton* (London: University of London Press, 1934).

83 Addy, Sidney Oldall, *Household tales with other traditional remains collected in the counties of York, Lincoln, Derby and Nottingham* (London: David Nutt, 1895), p.130.

84 Ibid.

85 Ibid., p.131.

86 University of Sheffield Special Collections ACT/97-003/2/5, Correspondence, Letter from Angela Barton, 8 July 1975.

87 Addy, Sidney Oldall, *Household tales with other traditional remains collected in the counties of York, Lincoln, Derby and Nottingham* (London: David Nutt, 1895), pp.132–33.

88 *High Peak News*, Thursday, 5 July 1883, p.5.

89 www.spacevoice.fsnet.co.uk/printro.htm, webpage now offline; accessed via archive.org 'Wayback Machine', 24 July 2022.

90 Ibid.

91 Ibid.

92 Ibid.

93 Ibid.

94 Ibid.

95 www.spacevoice.fsnet.co.uk/comms.htm, webpage now offline; accessed via archive.org 'Wayback Machine', 24 July 2022.

96 Addy, Sidney Oldall, *Household tales*

with other traditional remains collected in the counties of York, Lincoln, Derby and Nottingham (London: David Nutt, 1895), p.87.

97 Jewitt, W. Henry, C.C. Bell, and Mabel Peacock, 'Fifth of November Customs', *Folklore* 14, no. 2 (1903), pp.185–88.

98 Stubbs (1987), p.18.

99 University Of Sheffield Special Collections, Dave Bathe Collection, ACT/97-003/1/1/155, Edith Spencer letter, 20 March 1982.

100 Ibid.

101 Evans, Seth, *Bradwell: Ancient and Modern*, p.44.

102 Hallam, V.J., *Silent Valley: A History of the Derbyshire Villages of Ashopton and Derwent, now submerged beneath the Ladybower Dam* (Sheffield: Sheaf Publishing, 1983), p.2.

103 Quoted in Ibid., p.17.

104 The remains of Derwent village were also visible (to a lesser degree than in 1976 and 2018) following dry spells in both 1989 and 1995, and again in 2022.

105 Dickens, Charles, 'I Remember Arkwright', in Sadler, Geoffrey (ed.), *Aspects of Chesterfield* (Barnsley: Wharncliffe Books, 2002), p.70.

106 Ibid.

107 *Derbyshire Times*, Saturday, 1 July 1899, p.8.

108 *Derbyshire Advertiser and Journal*, Friday, 10 September 1858, p.7.

109 Ibid.

110 Porteous, Crichton, *The Beauty and Mystery of Well-dressing* (Derby: Pilgrim Press, 1949), p.103.

111 *Sheffield Daily Telegraph*, Tuesday, 3 May 1904, p.8.

112 Anon., Church of St James Brassington [church guide] ([Brassington: St James Church], n.d.), p.7.

113 sheelanagig.org/haddon-hall-derbyshire, accessed 10 May 2022.

114 www.youlgrave.org.uk, accessed 29 April 2022.

115 Ibid.

116 Bradbury, Edward, *All About Derbyshire* (1884), quoted in Wombwell, Margaret, *Ashover Remembered: Memories of Old Ashover* (Matlock: Derbyshire County Council Cultural & Community Services Department, 2005).

117 Wombwell, Margaret, *Ashover Remembered: Memories of Old Ashover* (Matlock: Derbyshire County Council Cultural & Community Services Department, 2005), pp.3–7.

118 Keeling, Jeremy (with Rick Broadbent), *Jeremy and Amy*, p.14.

119 Ibid., pp.14–15.

Bibliography

BOOKS

Addy, Sidney Oldall, *Household tales with other traditional remains collected in the counties of York, Lincoln, Derby and Nottingham* (London: David Nutt, 1895).

Anthony, Wayne, *Haunted Derbyshire and the Peak District* (Derby: Breedon Books, 1997).

Armitage, Jill, *Discover Celtic Derbyshire – 25 Walks* (Carmarthenshire: Sigma Leisure, 2013).

Armitage, Jill, *Traditional Derbyshire Fare – 300 recipes plus the stories and anecdotes behind them* (Carmarthenshire: Sigma Leisure, 2010).

Bailey, Stephen, *The Old Roads of Derbyshire: Walking into History: The Portway and Beyond* (Kibworth Beauchamp: Matador, 2019).

Bonsall Carnival Committee, *Celebrating 80 years of carnivals and well-dressings in Bonsall: from the 1920s to the 2000s* (Bonsall: Bonsall Carnival Committee, n.d.).

Bower, Alan, *Work and Play – from a Collection of Old Postcards of Derbyshire* (Derbyshire Heritage Series) (Derby: J.H. Hall and Sons Ltd., 1986).

Bradley, Richard, *Secret Chesterfield* (Stroud, Gloucestershire: Amberley, 2018).

Bradley, Richard, *Secret Matlock & Matlock Bath* (Stroud, Gloucestershire: Amberley, 2018).

Charlton, Christopher and Buxton, Doreen, *Matlock Bath: A Perfectly Romantic Place* (Matlock: Derwent Valley Mills World Heritage Site Educational Trust, 2019).

Clarke, David, *Supernatural Peak District* (London: Robert Hale, 2000).

Connole, Nellie, *Dark at Seven, The Life of a Derbyshire Miner: Being an account of his life as told by Joseph Sharpe of Coal Aston in the County of Derbyshire, 1859–1936* (York: Whitehead Books, 1988).

Drury, Jim, *'Fetch The Juicy Jam!' and other Memories of Birchover* (Birchover: The Reading Room, 2001).

Evans, Seth, *Bradwell: Ancient and Modern: history of the parish and incidents in the Hope Valley & District: being collections and recollections in a Peakland village* (Bradwell: Seth Evans, 1912).

Eyre, William J., *Strange North-East Derbyshire* (Dronfield: William J. Eyre, 2016).

Firth, J.B., *Highways and Byways In Derbyshire* (London: Macmillan and Co., 1908).

Goss, William Henry, *The Life and Death of Llewellynn Jewitt* (London: Henry
    Gray, 1889).

Greatorex, Michael, *Winster: People and Places in Postcards* (Little Longstone: Country
    Books, 2011).

Hallam, V.J., *Silent Valley: A History of the Derbyshire Villages of Ashopton and
    Derwent, now submerged beneath the Ladybower Dam* (Sheffield: Sheaf Publishing,
    1983).

Hannant, Sara, *Mummers, Maypoles and Milkmaids: A Journey Through the English
    Ritual Year* (London: Merrell, 2011).

Haywood, Barbara, *A Rake Through the Past: Memories of Middleton-by-Wirksworth*
    (Cromford: Barbara Haywood, 1996).

Jewitt, Llewellynn, *The Ballads & Songs of Derbyshire* (London: Bemrose &
    Lothian, 1867).

Keeling, Jeremy (with Rick Broadbent), *Jeremy and Amy* ([London]: Short Books,
    2010).

Maypole Promotions, *Milford and Makeney Milestones* (Milford: Maypole
    Promotions, 2002).

Miles, Clement A., *Christmas in Ritual and Tradition: Christian and Pagan* (London:
    Fisher Unwin, 1912).

Naylor, Peter, *Lost Villages of Derbyshire* (Derbyshire Heritage Series) (Darley
    Dale: Happy Walking International, 1997).

Porteous, Crichton, *The Ancient Customs of Derbyshire* (Derby: Derbyshire
    Countryside Ltd, 1976).

Porteous, Crichton, *The Beauty and Mystery of Well-dressing* (Derby: Pilgrim Press,
    1949).

Rickman, Philip & Nown, Graham, *Mysterious Derbyshire* (Clapham: Dalesman
    Books, 1977).

Severn, Joseph Millot, *My Village: Owd Codnor, Derbyshire, and the Village Folk
    when I Was a Boy* (Brighton: Joseph M. Severn, 1935).

Stoppard, Matthew Hedley, *The Garland King* (Scarborough: Valley Press, 2020).

Stubbs, Judith, *A History of Cutthorpe Village Part III: Besoms, Baskets and Black
    Gold* (Stubbs, Cutthorpe, 1987).

Tongue, Ruth, *Forgotten Folk-tales of the English Counties* (London: Routledge &
    Kegan Paul, 1970).

Toulson, Shirley, *Derbyshire: Exploring the Ancient Tracks and Mysteries of Mercia*
    (London: Wildwood House, 1980).

Uttley, Alison, *The Button-Box and Other Essays* (London: Faber and Faber, 1968).

Walker, W., *A History of Tideswell Including the Surrounding Villages* (Tideswell: W.
    Walker, 1951).

Wombwell, Margaret, *Ashover Remembered: Memories of Old Ashover* (Matlock:
    Derbyshire County Council Cultural & Community Services Department,
    2005).

ARTICLES

Brushfield, T., 'Reminiscences of Ashford-in-the-water, Sixty Years Ago', *The Reliquary* Vol. 6 (1865–66), pp.12–16.

Forrest-Lowe, M., 'The Naked Boys of Derbyshire', *Derbyshire Countryside* Vol. 31, No. 1 (January 1966), pp.40–41.

Jewitt, Llewellynn, 'On Ancient Customs and Sports of the County of Derby', *The Journal of The British Archaeological Association*, Vol. VIII (1852), pp.229–40.

Jewitt, W. Henry, C.C. Bell, and Mabel Peacock, 'Fifth of November Customs', *Folklore* Vol. 14, No. 2 (1903), pp.185–88.

Moore Smith, G.C., 'Bonfire night', *Notes and Queries*, Vol. s12-V, Issue 99 (December 1919), p.318.

Moutray Read, D.H., 'Hampshire Folklore', *Folklore* Vol. 22, No. 3 (1911), pp.292–329.

Russell, Ian, 'A Survey of Traditional Drama In North East Derbyshire 1970–78', *Folk Music Journal* Vol. 3 No. 5 (1979), pp.399–478.

Shipley, William J., 'Folk Dancing In Derbyshire', *The Derbyshire Countryside* Vol. 1 No. 4 (Oct 1931), pp.64–5.

Notts. & Derbyshire Notes and Queries, Vols. I–VI (1892–1898).

Anon., *Church of St James Brassington* [church guide] ([Brassington: St James Church], n.d.).

Leech, Chetwynd *'Our county town': An address delivered at a meeting of the London Society of Derbyshiremen at a Meeting of the Society at the Holborn Viaduct Hotel on February 15th, 1901* (London: The Columbus Company Limited, 1901).

Dickens, Charles, 'I Remember Arkwright', in Sadler, Geoffrey (ed.), *Aspects of Chesterfield* (Barnsley: Wharncliffe Books, 2002).

Flamsteed, John, 'Memoirs of Mr. John Flamsteed, by Himself' in Wright, Raymond, *Old stories and writings about Derbyshire: Culled from various almost forgotten sources and authors and put together for the first time in the hope that they will be thus preserved from oblivion* (Buxton: Borough of Buxton Public Library, 1933).

Lawrence, D.H., 'Wintry Peacock' in *England, My England* (Harmondsworth, Middlesex: Penguin Books, 1960).

Ramsbottom, Laurence, 'Folk Stories of Peakland', in *National Association of Head Teachers Conference Souvenir, Buxton* (London: University of London Press, 1934).

HISTORIC LOCAL NEWSPAPERS, AS CITED:

Ashbourne Telegraph
Belper New
Chester Courant
Derby Daily Telegraph
Derbyshire Advertiser and Journal

Derbyshire Courier
Derbyshire Times and Chesterfield Herald
Glossop Record
High Peak Chronicle
High Peak News

The Nottinghamshire Guardian
Morning Post
Sheffield Daily Telegraph
Sheffield Independent

WEBSITES

www.ancestry.co.uk/genealogy/records/anne-kendall-24-1bxjqv
traditionalcustomsandceremonies.com/2015/12/31/custom-revived-harthills-
    derby-tup
player.bfi.org.uk/free/film/watch-evidence-1935-online
archive.org/details/longago00unkngoog/page/n350
www.greatbritishlife.co.uk/things-to-do/whats-on/the-hen-racing-world-
    championships-in-bonsall-6499874
www.macearchive.org/films/central-news-east-01041986-hen-racing
www.crichparish.co.uk/webpages/kenyonhistory.html
www.scarthinbooks.com/authors-shakers/the-d-h-lawrence-gossip-column
movie-locations.com/movies/l/Living-Dead-At-Manchester-Morgue.php
woodlandschapel.wordpress.com
www.derbytelegraph.co.uk/burton/naked-man-said-took-clothes-3501442
chesterfield-observatory.co.uk/about/about-the-observatory
her.derbyshire.gov.uk/Monument/MDR3541
www.greatbritishlife.co.uk/homes-and-gardens/places-to-live/quarndon-s-
    fascinating-spa-resort-past-6512442
www.spacevoice.fsnet.co.uk/printro.htm
sheelanagig.org
www.youlgrave.org.uk

Here's a Health to the Barley Mow DVD, BFIVD920 (London: BFI, 2011).
'Twilight of the English Celts', *Chronicle*, BBC2, TX date 27 October 1977.

University of Sheffield Special Collections
97-015 – Dave Bathe Collection of Derbyshire Traditional Dance and Drama
ACT/97-003 – Charlotte Norman Derbyshire well dressing collection

The destination for history
www.thehistorypress.co.uk